MW01048141

Finding Money
for College

1996

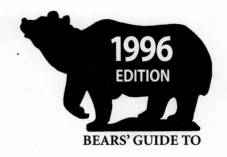

BEARS' GUIDE TO

Finding Money
for College

John Bear, Ph.D.

Mariah Bear, M.A.

Ten Speed Press
Berkeley, California

Copyright © 1996, 1993 by John B. Bear and Mariah P. Bear. Copyright © 1984 by John B. Bear. All rights reserved. No part of this book may be reproduced in any form, except brief excerpts for the purpose of review, without written permission of the publisher.

Ten Speed Press
Box 7123
Berkeley, California 94707

Cover design by Fifth Street Design
Interior design by Jeff Brandenburg, ImageComp

Printed in Canada

First printing, 1996

1 2 3 4 5 6 7 8 9 10 — 00 99 98 97 96

Distributed in Australia by E. J. Dwyer Pty. Ltd., in Canada by Publishers Group West, in New Zealand by Tandem Press, in South Africa by Real Books, and in the United Kingdom and Europe by Airlift Books.

Table of Contents

Acknowledgments

This book would not have been possible without the help of our diligent researchers: Joli Kornzweig, who spent many sunny days holed up in libraries around the Bay digging up weird and wonderful scholarships, and the ace backup phone team, Christa Laib and Kelly Newton, who insured that the information in this book is as accurate as humanly possible.

In addition, we'd like to thank Susannah Bear for her astute editorial comments, Jeff Brandenburg for his wonderful interior design, and Fifth Street for a fabulous cover.

At Ten Speed, we thank Hal Hershey for his supernatural patience with our missed deadlines and flimsy excuses, and Kirsty Melville, George Young, and Phil Wood for their unwavering support throughout the process.

And, as ever, thank you to Marina and to Joe . . . you make it all worthwhile.

A Bit of Inspiration
Before You Begin

I've Never Tried It Because I Don't Like It

That bit of poignant philosophy was the slogan of the Guinness Stout people in England some years ago. Their market research had shown them that many people were so sure they knew exactly what the stuff would taste like, they felt no need to actually try it. But the market research *also* showed that once people *did* sample the brew, they often liked it.

How often does the same erroneous point of view creep into your life? How many parents have said (or thought), "I don't *have* to ask you—I already *know* the answer." How many tennis players have assumed, "No point in running for that shot; I'd never get there." How many lovers, contest entrants, authors . . .

. . . and how many impoverished students (or would-be students) have failed to seek funds from various sources because they decided in advance that they had no chance of success?

So, remember those billions of unclaimed dollars out there, pay close attention to the "return on your investment" philosophy, and (if it still makes sense for you) *go for it.*

Important Issues

Chapter
1

Why This Book Is Needed

There are dozens of books and reports on the subject of financing a college education. We have examined virtually every one of them—those sold in bookstores, those sold by mail, and the out-of-print and rare ones available only in libraries.

They all seem to have one major flaw, and most have two major omissions. These three basic problems render them almost useless for many readers in many situations.

The Major Flaw

In three words, *lack of creativity*. The existing literature—and indeed, the usual advice given by financial aid counselors at high-schools and colleges—plows the same overworked ground—over and over and over.

Federal aid. State aid. The major scholarship funds. Work-study programs . . . and precious little more.

There's nothing wrong with those options, but they represent only a fraction of the available techniques—and the available funds.

It is a tragic fact that every year, hundreds of thousands of students drop out of school, fail to go to college, or end up at a poorer school than the one they really wanted, solely because they were not given financial advice that was correct, comprehensive, *and* creative.

Major Omission #1

Without exception, the books are written primarily for high-school seniors (and their parents).

There's nothing wrong with this—except that roughly half of the people going to college these days are older people who have taken anywhere from one to sixty years "off" to pursue other matters before carrying on with their formal education.

Major Omission #2

The primary focus of these other books is the problem of finding money to pay for a traditional four-year residential Bachelor's degree.

But a high percentage of people with money problems are interested in Master's degrees, Doctorates, part-time study, night school, law and medical degrees, other professional training, Bible schools, and so forth.

Chapter 2

Why This Book Is Out of Date Already and Why That's All Right

No reference book can be as up-to-date as the readers (or the authors) would like. It is a fact of life that facts change. Names, addresses, policies, dollar amounts, telephone numbers, and other data are always in flux.

So there are bound to be errors in this book, for which we apologize in advance. The most frequent cause of error is that the rules and regulations affecting government programs are almost constantly undergoing changes and reinterpretations. The next most common cause is that foundations change the amounts of money they have available or their giving policies. Starving students one year, displaced homemakers the next. And then there are the annoying but unavoidable changes in addresses and telephone numbers.

The good news is that at any given time, 90 to 95 percent of the facts in this book will be correct and some of the rest will still be close. Please don't get too mad at a batter with a .900 average.

And please help us make the 1997 edition even more accurate by sharing with us any errors, changes, omissions, or other matters you discover that you think should be changed. Thank you very much.

You can reach us at this address:

John B. Bear and Mariah P. Bear
P.O. Box 7123-F
Berkeley, CA 94707

Four Things You Need to Know Before You Begin Your Quest

1. It's a Buyer's Market Out There

Somehow most people find it hard to conceive of a university as a business, much less a business that has a real possibility of failure in hard economic times.

Enlightened colleges and universities follow a business model very closely. They know that if enrollments (sales) are down, there can be major cash flow problems. They worry about the size of their endowment (assets). They pay close attention to advertising, marketing their services, and public relations.

But most schools are *not* enlightened and a remarkable number are in genuine financial trouble. Indeed, over the last few years, a college or university has gone out of business (closed down, or merged into another school to escape its creditors) on an average of *once every three weeks.*

That's why it's a buyer's market out there. Like the desperate car dealer who would rather sell a car for a $100 profit than lose a sale entirely, many schools will go far out of their way to lure you into their fold.

After all, they well know that it costs them almost nothing to put one more student into an otherwise partly empty dormitory room or lecture hall. They've got to meet the payroll, the mortgage payment, and the utility bills—all of which remain virtually constant whether the schools are operating at 80 percent of capacity or 100 percent. So each additional student who enrolls and pays even *some* tuition is pure gravy for the school.

Some people may feel uncomfortable "bargaining" with a university over tuition, fees, and terms of payment. But it is not at all an unreasonable thing to do in these times.

We don't mean to imply that an admissions officer and a potential student should go at it like stereotypical rug merchants. Matters can be handled in quite a dignified manner. The school is probably even more uncomfortable stepping out of the "traditional" academic mold than the student, and will gladly seek creative solutions that enable it to save face. Indeed, most "tuition reduction grants" or "partial tuition scholarships" are simply the school saying, in a dignified way, "All right, you say $6,000 is too much to pay. I'll tell ya what I'm gonna do. I'm gonna knock two big ones off the bottom line and only charge you four G's . . ."

We are convinced that many old-line schools (in the person of their admissions or financial aid officers) would rather go discreetly bankrupt than feel that they had descended to the level of the bazaar. But they *are* more than likely to be willing to listen to the potential student who says, in effect:

1. The amount of money involved may present a problem for me.
2. I am well aware that there are many other similar institutions, and I may have to investigate them to see if they may be able to offer creative alternatives—or listen to mine.

The really important thing to remember about this is that it is *really all right to do so.* You may feel a little uncomfortable. The school may feel a little uncomfortable. But the bottom line is that a great deal of money may be saved.

Bear in mind, too, that at most colleges and universities, tuition accounts for only about one-third of the total amount necessary for running the school. The rest comes from their endowment (their assets, in effect: money, real estate, and other investments, etc.), gifts from alumni and others, grants from foundations and corporations, and Good Ol' Uncle Sam.

As a result of this, many schools set their tuition rates abnormally high to avoid providing scholarships for the rich. In other words, they reason that rich students may as well pay a higher portion of the cost of running the school, while they *fully expect the less-rich applicants to pay a good deal less.*

2. The Matter of Merit versus Need

Let us say that a university has one place left in its entering class, and there are two applicants. Applicant #1 has a good solid B+ average, pretty good test scores, pretty good letters of reference, and a million dollars. Applicant #2 has an A average, extremely high test scores, fantastic letters of reference, and is flat broke.

Who is admitted? Let's complicate the matter just a little by adding the fact that the school is facing possibly severe financial problems a year or two down the road.

Should they "accept" the $10,000 from the rich kid, or should they *offer* a $1,000 scholarship to the poor kid?

There is no simple or consistent answer. Some schools feel it is most important to lure the best possible students, regardless of the consequences. Some of these argue that it makes sense, given the grand long-range picture, to go for the best, because schools with Rhodes Scholars, famous alumni, and Nobel Laureates are more likely, way down the road, to get larger grants and donations . . . if they survive that long. Others feel that having rich or influential alumni may be a school's best asset.

Other schools have convinced themselves, generally accurately, that there isn't *that* much correlation between predicted performance and actual performance. The B+ applicant may well turn out to be a better student—and his or her money could *remove* the straw and *save* the camel's back.

And some schools are masters of compromise. They install some double bunks in the dormitories, some extra chairs in the lecture halls, and admit *both* students.

When foundations and other scholarship-grantors face this merit-versus-need problem, their solution is often to award *both* applicants a scholarship, but one gets honor plus money, the other honor alone. It is not uncommon for a top applicant with substantial financial resources to be told, "Congratulations! You are one of two recipients of the Millard Fillmore Memorial Scholarship. The other recipient will be getting the entire $10,000, while you will receive a hearty handshake and a glorious certificate on genuine parchment."

3. A Remarkable Amount of Money Is Unclaimed Each Year

So-called authorities differ mightily on the exact amount, but they all agree that a very large amount of money that *could* be spent on college scholarships, if only someone had asked, goes unclaimed every year simply because no one did ask.

The various estimates range from as "little" as several hundred million dollars to as much as seven billion dollars. The reason for the disparity is that it is not always clear whether certain money would have been spent if someone *had* asked for it.

For example, thousands of corporations have programs in which they will pay for all or part of their employees' school expenses. Based on what the corporations *say* they would have done, over six billion dollars in tuition and fee reimbursement goes unclaimed each year, simply because no one asked for it. This is partly because school-attending employees are unaware of the reimbursement plan, and partly because not enough employees choose to attend school in their spare time. (This is discussed further in Chapter 9.)

Another example: There are hundreds of foundations that make grants for "general educational and philanthropic purposes"—which *could* include school expenses if people applied for them—but surprisingly few people actually do this.

A final example: Even though private colleges and universities are frequently willing to "negotiate" tuition and fees, often, as indicated, the school feels uncomfortable entering the marketplace in this way, and the potential student doesn't know that this option is available. Thus additional millions of dollars, in the form of tuition reductions, go unclaimed.

4. There Are an Awful Lot of Very Tiny Awards Out There

Thousands and thousands of foundations, schools, and scholarship schemes specialize in cash grants of $25, $50, $100, and thereabouts. Now we must applaud their charitable intent, but the actual usefulness of the gift, other than as an honor that looks good on a resumé or admissions application, is minimal indeed. (John is, for instance, the holder of the Bausch and Lomb Scholarship, given to two graduating seniors at his high school. Twenty-five bucks and a certificate with his name typed in. As he recalls, he and a few friends took the money and went out to a Bausch and Lomb Commemorative Lunch.)

Many books on scholarships, and many of the reports provided by scholarship search services, will be "bulked out" with these almost trivial matters.

But unless the honor is really important, for whatever psychological reasons, it generally does not make sense to invest much time and energy in an application that may result, at best, in a two-figure grant. This subject is explored in Chapter 4, dealing with return on investment.

In the course of this book, then, we have pretty well ignored the little fellows. Of course $100 is nothing to sneeze at—but with a fixed amount of money-seeking time, there are almost certainly more efficient places to sneeze.

Return on Investment: How Much Time and Effort Should You Spend in Your Quest?

"Return on investment" means the amount you get back, in relation to the amount you put in. If you were running a manufacturing business and got back $117 for every $100 you spent, you'd be doing all right. If you got back $83 for every $100 spent, you'd be well advised to do something different.

In the matter of questing after money for college, it makes sense to consider both the financial and the psychological return on investment.

Financial Return on Investment

There are certain costs involved in applying for scholarships, fellowships, grants, and the like. Out-of-pocket costs (postage, telephone calls, preparing resumes, portfolios, travel, etc.) are generally quite low for each separate application—but if twenty or thirty or more separate applications are being made, the total amount can be substantial. If the value of your time is factored in—and perhaps it should be, especially if you could be out *earning* money during the time you spend *applying* for money—you may even find that the potential return on your investment is not large enough to make it worth your while.

Once, when John was a teacher earning $12 an hour, he decided to apply for a fellowship from a large foundation. Preparing the complex application required about fifty hours and $200 in various expenses. Thus his cost was either $800 (time and money) or $200 (money only).

He learned later (after being declined) that about one out of every seventy-seven applications received a grant of about $12,000. Thus, if others' expenses were comparable to his, the total investment of seventy-seven applicants was $61,000 (time and money) or $15,000 (money only) for this $12,000 sum. In either case, not a great investment, taken as a group.

From John's individual standpoint, the financial argument was this: Is it worth investing money when there is one chance in seventy-seven that I will get back sixty times my investment? Financially, of course not. Psychologically, another story indeed, as any visitor to Las Vegas or Atlantic City, participant in the Publishers Clearinghouse Sweepstakes, or buyer of a state lottery ticket will readily attest.

We don't want to denigrate in any way the excellent work of the American Legion in providing scholarships and other financial awards to hundreds of worthy high school seniors each year, largely through public speaking and essay contests. But the amount of time and energy required to participate in these contests, with the potential of a $100 or $500 (in most cases) scholarship, cannot be considered an outstanding financial decision. A good return on financial investment? No. On psychological investment? Maybe. Read on.

Psychological Return on Investment

No one who enters a big national sweepstakes *really* expects to win. Still, the thinking goes, someone has to win, so why not me? If it only requires a few minutes of my time, and one postage stamp, why not take the chance and indulge in the fantasy of thinking about the big prizes, and what I would do if . . .

Many aspiring authors go through the same process. Some have sent the manuscript of their novel off to a hundred or more publishers, probably spending more in time and postage than their royalties would be even if it was published. But as long as it is "out there" being considered, there is hope, and that hope sustains the creative flame and makes ordinary life just a little more pleasant.

So it is with applications for money. From our communications with hundreds of would-be college students of all ages, it is now clear to us that the *very act* of pursuing money often has a good effect on the life of the student, *whether or not the money comes.*

Person after person has told us that while they were in the process of making one or more applications, two quite unexpected side effects became apparent:

1. The planning, thought, and preparation that went into the application process helped them to clarify their own educational goals, often with positive effects in deciding exactly what classes, majors, and even thesis or dissertation topics to pursue; and

2. The very act of preparing the application—the time spent immersed in a combination of plans and fantasies—so fired their enthusiasm that they became absolutely determined to pursue their educational goals no matter what—and often found a way to do it, even before they heard from the money-dispensing agency to which they had applied.

What conclusion can be drawn? The only one, really, is this: Let the end (or potential end) justify the means. Assess your chances as carefully as you can, estimate the time and expense of applying as carefully as you can (bearing in mind that a second application may make use of much of the material prepared for the first, and thus can be much less expensive), and make a largely rational decision based on your own assessment (for no one can do it for you) of the probable rate of return on your financial and psychological investment.

And finally, there may well be some "pyramiding" effects, in which the gatekeepers to one source of money will be impressed by the actions of another set of gatekeepers. For instance, the very act of winning a quite modest $200 in an American Legion oratorical contest may attract the attention of the people who dispense large scholarships or loan funds on behalf of other organizations.

Six Strategies for Saving Money

Advanced Entrance

For the Bachelor's degree, you can save one to three years by starting at an advanced level, either through credit for examination, for work done previously, or for life experience learning credit. Advanced placement is discussed in Chapter 20. The nontraditional schools covered in Chapter 19 specialize in this kind of thing.

Early Entrance

One Bear family member, Susannah, decided, when she simultaneously reached the age of sixteen and the end of tenth grade, that she had learned just about everything high school had to teach her. Her old parents were not initially thrilled with her plan to "drop out" and take the high school equivalency exam (which is offered by all fifty states).

Susannah passed, enrolled as a college freshman, and saved her family two years' worth of the cost of supporting her. Good on yer, Susannah.

Skipping two years is unusual, but one year is quite common, and so, for younger people, the notion of abandoning high school early and heading off to college is well worth considering.

What are the disadvantages? A primary one seems to be missing high school graduation. But not necessarily. Mariah, coauthor of this book, followed a similar plan of action. She found a college that would admit her early, without either the equivalency exam *or* the diploma. After a year at college, she flew home for a couple of days to take part in the graduation ceremonies of the class she would have been part of. The airline ticket cost was inconsequential compared with the cost of sustaining a hungry teenager for an additional year.

Guaranteed Tuition

With tuition generally rising faster than the rate of inflation, it is safe to assume that today's typical $6,000 annual tuition bite will be closer to $8,000 or $9,000 by the end of an undergraduate program.

A few schools offer a guarantee that the tuition will remain the same for a given student—undergraduate or graduate—until the degree is earned.

Some schools that don't *officially* make such an offer may still be willing to consider it, as part of the financial negotiations preceding your decision to enroll.

A few schools "allow" students to prepay the entire tuition for the years they are going to be enrolled. It is hard to imagine that anyone clever enough to amass the very large sum of money necessary to do this would actually fall for such a scheme.

And what, a few may ask, if tuition rates come down? What if Earth is destroyed by the Asparagus People from Jupiter? Equal likelihood.

Start Simple, End Fancy

Some people whose *real* goal is, say, a Harvard degree, but who cannot manage the $80,000 or more it would take, elect do their first year or two at the local cheap (or free) college, and *then* transfer to the fancy one for the last two years.

While Harvard and some other well-known institutions require a minimum of two years on campus, many universities only insist on one year. John's Bachelor's degree, for instance, is from the University of California at Berkeley, where he spent only two semesters, having transferred in from another school for his senior year only.

Pay Tuition Without Money

Barter is alive and well in the academic marketplace. See Chapter 11 for a discussion of how it can be used.

Choose a Nontraditional Program

In a companion volume, *College Degrees by Mail*, we describe 100 nontraditional schools and programs, where it is possible to earn good, usable degrees without sitting in classes and lecture halls full time.

It is, indeed, honestly possible to earn Bachelor's, Master's, Doctorates, and even law degrees entirely through correspondence study, or with only very short occasional visits to the campus. Full details in Chapter 19.

Getting Money

Getting Money from Private Foundations

Foundations are organizations established by individuals and/or corporations as a means to dispense money and, often, to help others. Often there are tax considerations, in that foundations are started using funds that might otherwise go to the Internal Revenue Service.

There are well over 100,000 foundations in America, with assets ranging from under $100 to over $1 billion. While many foundations have very specific stated purposes which are of no relevance to this book (such as "to repair roofs of Baptist churches" or "to build playgrounds in parks"), many others have goals that are not specifically defined. A common one is "to support educational, scientific, religious, and other charitable needs."

There are two basic approaches to getting money from these private charitable foundations.

1. Foundations with Formal Scholarship Procedures

There are foundations—some large, many small—with formal procedures for applying for college money. Most have specific deadlines and rigid methods for choosing the recipients (test scores, essays, etc.). For example, the Sachs Foundation awards hundreds of thousands of dollars for college costs each year to African Americans who live in Colorado.

2. Foundations with Informal or Unstructured Procedures

An intriguing, little-known, and little-used source of money is the private charitable foundation that does *not* have well-established scholarship programs—indeed, they often have none at all.

These foundations frequently have nonspecific charitable purposes, enabling them to give money each year to causes as diverse as medical research, a fund to put flowers on veterans' graves, and paying the university tuition for a dozen worthy students.

Foundations can also be divided into two categories by another important factor: those that make grants to individual human beings, and those that only give money to organizations.

No problems in dealing with those in the first group. But the second, representing more than 90 percent of all foundations, should not be written off. There is a strategy that has been successfully used many times, in which individuals end up with funds from foundations that cannot, by terms of their charter or policies of their founders, give money to individual. This strategy is described in detail beginning on page 22.

The Large "Traditional Scholarship" Foundations

Many of them are well known to high school counselors and to financial aid officers at colleges and universities. They are also covered in detail in the book *Foundation Grants to Individuals* described on page 24. We describe some of the major ones later in this chapter, but in general pay less attention to them, since they are really so easy to learn about and deal with through the prescribed formula means.

The Less Traditional Foundations, or Those without a Specific Scholarship Program

The key factor to know about here is that the people who run these foundations—the ones who make the decisions about who gets how much—are often bored. They are bored because the vast majority of their applications are essentially the same.

Now there's nothing wrong with worthy causes like hospital-building funds, opera guilds, Christmas baskets for the needy, and missionary support societies. But if you were the person (or committee) in charge of making financial decisions for a foundation, and each year you got dozens (or hundreds) or almost-identical money requests from almost-identical organizations, might you not crave (and eagerly respond to) requests from creative and interesting-sounding people for unusual projects?

We have talked to the decision makers at a number of foundations, ranging from the very small (under $10,000 a year in grants) to the very large (over $10 million a year). Many of them agree that an unusual "special" application or request stands out from the others like a unicorn in a herd of goats.

Here are just a few examples:

One very large foundation had developed something of a reputation as a supporter of homes for single mothers. This foundation's new director decided that only half of the millions each year would go to that cause, and the other half would go to "really interesting stuff." Soon after, an application came in from a graduate student who wanted tuition plus funding for his research in parapsychology. He described some of the experiments he had performed, and the ones he had in mind. The foundation was enchanted, and paid him more than $20,000 a year for his three years of graduate school.

A very small foundation found, among its standard "Here's why I want you to pay my tuition" letters, a charming proposal from a young married student who was concerned that if his wife became pregnant, he might have to drop out of school. He asked only for a few hundred dollars to buy birth control pills for the duration of his studies. Granted.

An applicant who phrased her tuition request in the form of a long and lovely narrative poem on the beauties of her native region, and how important it was for her to study there and remain there, received the foundation's largest single grant of the year—"As much to reward her for her beautiful writing as to finance her further education," they reported.

An applicant who was an accomplished woodworker, and wanted to enroll in a business school to learn how to capitalize on his skills, sent a small piece of furniture along with his application, which truly impressed the decision-making committee.

And so it goes. Undoubtedly there are many rigid and humorless foundations which are not at all impressed by creative or unusual applications (which they regard as frivolous). But (bearing in mind the "return on investment" factors discussed in Chapter 4) it can do no harm to attempt to bring some delight into the lives of these decision makers—who may, in turn, bring some delightful money into yours.

How Individuals Can Deal with Foundations That Won't or Can't Deal with Individuals

Approximately 95 percent of foundations are either unable (because of their charters) or unwilling (because of their current policies) to deal with individual human beings. They give their money only to organizations—frequently, only not-for-profit organizations.

The money, however, *always* ends up being used by individuals—whether the cancer research physician, the single mother who stays at home, the starving child in Africa, or the student attending the college that was given the money.

Sometimes it is possible to orchestrate the act of giving so that the money is given to an *organization* which has agreed in advance to use the money for a specific human being.

For instance, a student required funds to pursue a Master's degree in audiology. When she discovered that most of the foundations interested in hearing research don't give money to individuals, she approached several universities with good programs in speech and hearing, and proposed that she work with them to write a grant proposal to certain foundations. The money received would support the particular research in which she would participate. In other words, the foundation would give the money to the university, and the university would (directly or indirectly) use the money for her tuition and other expenses.

It is also possible to pursue a three-step approach, instead of the two-step one.

A student wished to study physical education, with special attention to sports medicine and physiology. He approached a medical group specializing in this field, and worked with them in developing a grant proposal. When the money came to the medical group, they used most of it to pay for the student's tuition at a nearby school, and the balance to pay his salary as a part-time assistant in their research.

Some foundations that cannot give to individuals are willing and eager to participate in these kinds of two- and three-step processes—either because they see it as a logical interpretation of the guidelines, or because the administrators of the foundation feel constrained and restricted by their guidelines. Other foundations see it as a subversion of the process, and may even ask for an assurance that any money given will not be used in this manner.

The important guideline here is that you should not automatically reject those 95 percent of foundations that don't give to individuals. If you have contacts at a relevant organization (preferably a nonprofit one that could receive foundation funds), or are willing to seek them out, you may wish to consider the 95 percent as well as the 5 percent.

Where and How to Learn About Foundations

There are 4 outstanding locations, and 125 pretty good locations, to consult for information. There is a list of relevant foundations beginning on page 26. And there are some relevant books and a computerized information service providing specific facts and figures, names and addresses.

The Four Outstanding Locations

There is a splendid national organization called The Foundation Center, which is financed by some foundations, and which maintains immense amounts of information on more than 22,000 currently active foundations.

As their literature aptly points out, "it takes serious, often time-consuming, research to track down those [foundations] with giving records or stated objectives that are related to your [interests]." The Foundation Center receives Internal Revenue Service returns for more than 19,000 smaller and 3,000 larger foundations, showing just what they did in the last year. They also have scads of annual reports, press releases and newsletters, sample application forms, reference books, indices and cross-indices to subject areas, and useful data on other sources of funding (government, corporations, other agencies).

The Foundation Center maintains its materials and offers its services in four locations, each of which is comfortable, well-equipped with copying and microform facilities, and, most significantly, staffed by knowledgeable and helpful librarians—and all of this with no cost to the user.

The four locations are:

79 Fifth Avenue, betw. 15th and 16th
New York, NY 10003
(212) 620-4230

1001 Connecticut Avenue NW, Suite 938
Washington, DC 20036
(202) 331-1400

312 Sutter Street
San Francisco, CA 94108
(415) 397-0902

422 Euclid Avenue, Room 1356
Cleveland, OH 44114
(216) 861-1934

The 125 Pretty Good Locations

The very same Foundation Center also maintains more limited collections of relevant material, located in 125 "host libraries"—public, university, and government libraries. Here can be found major reference works, and specific data on foundations within the state or region.

There are host libraries in each of the fifty states, as well as in Canada, Mexico, Puerto Rico, and the Virgin Islands.

Rather than use a lot of space listing all 125 (when at least 124 will not be of interest to any given reader), let me just suggest that you call the Foundation Center's toll-free number, and they will be pleased to give you the location of the library nearest you.

The number is (800) 424-9836.

Some Relevant Books

Foundation Grants to Individuals is a useful book compiled by Claude Barilleaux and Alexis Gersunky, published and sold by The Foundation Center.

It describes nearly 1,000 of the large foundations that make grants to individuals: name, address, phone, financial data (assets, amount granted last year), fields of interest, deadlines, sample grants made, etc.

These foundations each year grant over $100 million to more than 50,000 individuals.

The 500-plus-page book may be consulted free at the libraries described above, or purchased directly from The Foundation Center, 79 Fifth Avenue, New York, NY 10003. The price is $65. Credit card orders can be made on the toll-free phone line, (800) 424-9836.

Where the Money's At by Irving Warner and Patricia Tobey is a clever and inspirational book whose usefulness has, sadly, declined because it is out of date. Mr. Warner is one of America's best-known fund-raisers, and author of the standard text on the subject, *The Art of Fund Raising.* He and Ms. Tobey scoured the public disclosure records of every one of the thousands of charitable donors in California and selected 525 representative ones. Each of these is described in some detail, including the particulars of specific grants made in recent years.

That's where the inspirational part comes in. Reading through all these descriptions, it is hard *not* to think of an academic or educational project that seems compatible.

Very few of the listed grants are to individuals—but that's not necessarily significant, as described earlier.

The book was compiled in 1978, so most of the specific information is no longer accurate or relevant. (A new edition is being contemplated, if a publisher will step forward.) The age in no way detracts from the inspirational value. And there is a most useful essay by Mr. Warner on how to (and how *not* to) approach foundations.

To summarize his advice:

1. Be sensible and thoughtful. Don't send form letters. Don't write to foundations whose stated interests are far from your own.
2. Play hunches. Nothing to be lost by trying.
3. Be brief and clear in making the initial inquiry—no more than a page and a half.
4. Avoid obvious gimmicks—paper butterflies that flutter out when the letter is opened; letters in pencil on paper bags.
5. Follow up, politely, if you haven't had a response or acknowledgment within two weeks.
6. Keep trying. Be persistent; be creative.

The Foundation Directory is the standard reference book on foundations, issued every couple of years by The Foundation Center. In 1,945 large pages, it describes more than 4,000 corporate, community, and independent foundations: virtually every foundation in the U.S. with assets over $1 million and/or annual grants over $100,000. The directory describes the interests, financial data, and specific application information. It can be found in many public libraries, and is available from The Foundation Center for $175.

Corporate Foundation Profiles offers an extremely detailed description of the 230 largest company-sponsored foundations, plus short descriptions of 400 additional such foundations. They may be of special relevance since many corporate foundations have interests directly related to the company's products or services. Thus students (or would-be students) of chemistry, for instance, might pay special attention to the foundations sponsored by one or another of the major chemical manufacturers.

The book is revised regularly, and sold by The Foundation Center for $145.

Foundation Grants Index Annual is published each year by The Foundation Center, which studies the annual reports of hundreds of large foundations and creates a subject index to tens of thousands of their grants to organizations—including those as small as $5,000. The two main values of this approach are in locating foundations that are active in very specific fields of endeavor, and in learning which nonprofit organizations are successful in getting grants. The 2,122-page volume sells for $150.

Scholarships with Few or No Strings Attached

Teya Albertani Foundation for Involvement, Inc., 853 North SR 434, Altamonte Springs, FL 32714

> *Two grants of $2,500 each for students who have shown outstanding leadership qualities and have excelled in their involvement in school and community activities.*

Coca-Cola Scholars Foundation, One Buckhead Plaza, Suite 1000, 3060 Peachtree Road, NW, Atlanta, GA 30305

> *Over $1.4 million to 150 high school seniors based on leadership, academic performance, and activities.*

Earhart Foundation, 2200 Green Road, Suite H, Ann Arbor, MI 48105

> *Over $1.3 million in research grants to individuals "who have distinguished themselves professionally."*

Educational Communications Scholarship Foundation, 721 North McKinley Road, Lake Forest, IL 60045

> *Scholarships to mature students who have demonstrated ability and effort.*

The Ford Foundation, 320 East 43rd Street, New York, NY 10017

> *Grants totaling $3.4 million for advanced research in the fields of human rights, education and culture, and international affairs.*

The Freedom Forum International, Inc., 1101 Wilson Boulevard, Arlington, VA 22091

> *Fellowships and scholarships totaling $1.5 million for journalists and students.*

Fannie and John Hertz Foundation, Box 5032, Livermore, CA 94551-5032

> *Over $2.3 million in grants to graduate students in the sciences, and to high school graduates from the San Francisco Bay Area.*

Humane Studies Foundation, 4084 University Drive, Suite 101, Fairfax, VA 22030

> *Research grants and fellowships in any area of knowledge, with emphasis on the social sciences.*

John Miskoff Foundation, 9605 North East 79th Avenue, No. 16, Hialeah Gardens, FL 33016

> *Seven loans totaling $31,000 to individuals who have completed their sophomore year of college.*

The Bill Raskob Foundation, Inc., P.O. Box 4019, Wilmington, DE 19807

> *One hundred eighteen interest-free loans totaling $184,400, for U.S. citizens whose work toward a degree is already underway.*

The Rockefeller Foundation, 420 Fifth Avenue, New York, NY 10018-2702
Nearly $7 million in grants to promote graduate study and research in a variety of fields.

Leopold Schepp Foundation, 551 Fifth Avenue, Suite 3000, New York, NY 10176
Grants totaling $626,000 to students who need financial assistance in order to complete their education.

Hattie M. Strong Foundation, 1620 I Street NW, Suite 700, Washington, DC 20006
Interest-free loans totaling $498,850 to 251 U.S. citizens in their final year of an undergraduate or graduate program.

Tyson Foundation, Inc., 2210 Oaklawn, Springdale, AR 72762
Grants totaling $342,710 to students majoring in business, agriculture, engineering, computer science, or nursing.

Kathryn M. Whitten Trust, c/o Farmers & Merchants Trust Company, P.O. Box 891, Long Beach, CA 90801
Twenty-four grants totaling $59,800 to students maintaining a B average.

Youth Activities Director of Americanism, National Headquarters of the American Legion, P.O. Box 1055, Indianapolis, IN 46206-1055
Awards of up to $18,000 each to winners of an oratorical contest.

Scholarships Linked to Area of Study

Arts

Frank Huntington Beebe Fund for Musicians, c/o Welch and Forbes, 45 School Street, Boston, MA 02108
Seven grants totaling $37,780 to finance study abroad for talented musicians and painters.

James Hubert Blake Trust, c/o Beldock, Levine, and Hoffman, 99 Park Avenue, Suite 1600, New York, NY 10016-1502
Fifteen music scholarships totaling $36,450, particularly for students interested in traditional American ragtime music.

Dog Writers Educational Trust, P.O. Box 2220, Payson, AZ 85547
Ten grants of $1,000 each to students who have a background in organized dog activities.

William Randolph Hearst Foundation, 90 New Montgomery Street, Suite 1212, San Francisco, CA 94105

Awards totaling $288,000 to undergraduates in an accredited journalism program.

Samuel H. Kress Foundation, 174 East 80th Street, New York, NY 10021

Seventy-four grants totaling $467,350 for graduate study in art history.

National Scholarship Trust Fund, Education Council, Graphic Arts Industry, 4615 Forbes Avenue, Pittsburgh, PA 15213

Scholarships totaling $350,000 to students pursuing a career in graphics communications.

The Poynter Fund, P.O. Box 625, St. Petersburg, FL 33731-0625

Grants totaling $95,630 for undergraduate and graduate study of journalism.

Scripps Howard Foundation, P.O. Box 5380, Cincinnati, OH 45201

Over 300 scholarships totaling $350,750 for students pursuing careers in print or broadcast journalism.

Political Science

The J. Edgar Hoover Foundation, 50 Gull Point Road, Hilton Head Island, SC 29928

Thirty-one grants totaling $31,900, for the study of government and good citizenship.

Science

The Howard Hughes Medical Institute, c/o Office of Grants and Special Programs, 4000 Jones Bridge Road, Chevy Chase, MD 20815-6789

Over $16 million in grants for predoctoral and postdoctoral research fellowships in the biological and medical sciences.

The Charles A. and Anne Morrow Lindbergh Foundation, 708 South Third Street, Suite 110, Minneapolis, MN 55415-1141

Ten grants totaling $94,741 for research and educational projects addressing the balance between technology and the environment.

Rob and Bessie Welder Wildlife Foundation, P.O. Box 1400, Sinton, TX 78387

Twenty grants totaling $171,319 to promote graduate-level study and research in the area of wildlife conservation.

Religious Studies

The Modglin Family Foundation, 7411 Lorge Circle, Huntington Beach, CA 92647

Fifty-three grants totaling $355,646 for students attending southern California theological seminaries.

The Numata Center for Buddhist Translation and Research, 2620 Warring Street, Berkeley, CA 94704

Grants totaling $30,438 for Buddhist studies.

Social Science

Wenner-Gren Foundation for Anthropological Research, Inc., 220 Fifth Avenue, 16th Floor, New York, NY 10001

Over $1.5 million in fellowships and research grants to anthropology scholars.

Scholarships Linked to Gender

AEI Scholarship Fund, c/o Society Bank, 100 South Main Street, Ann Arbor, MI 48104

Two grants of $4,226 each to female medical students.

CSU Forgivable Loan/Doctoral Incentive Program

See listing under Resources for Students with Disabilities

Maud Glover Folsom Foundation, Inc., 10 North Road, Harwinton, CT 06791

Sixty-five grants from $1,250 to $2,500 each, for male students of American ancestry and of Anglo-Saxon or German descent, between the ages of fourteen and twenty.

Helen Wegman Parmelee Educational Foundation, 1547 Lakeside Drive, Oakland, CA 94612

Eight grants of $3,500 each to female undergraduates.

Spence Reese Foundation, Boys Club of San Diego, 2930 Marcy Avenue, San Diego, CA 92113

Thirty-two grants of $1,000 each awarded to males in their senior year of high school, planning to major in medicine, law, engineering, or political science.

The Karla Scherer Foundation, 100 Renaissance Center, Suite 1680, Detroit, MI 48243-1009

Twenty-six grants totaling $60,500 to women pursuing graduate or undergraduate degrees in business.

The Thanks Be to Grandmother Winifred Foundation, P.O. Box 1449, Wainscott, NY 11975

Thirty-five grants totaling $105,397 to women over the age of fifty-four to pursue goals, including further education, which empower and enrich the lives of women.

Scholarships Linked to Ethnic or Cultural Background

Scholarship Programs for Native Americans

Many universities, some states, and numerous foundations, churches, and other organizations offer scholarships specifically for Native Americans. (A Native American is usually defined as a person who is at least one-fourth American Indian, Eskimo, or Aleut, and is recognized as such by his or her tribe. The tribe, in turn, must be one recognized by the Bureau of Indian Affairs.)

Said Bureau has consolidated all of the relevant information on available scholarships, fellowships, career-training opportunities, and other useful material into a fifty-six-page book called *Opportunities for Native Americans.* It is available from the Scholarship Office, Bureau of Indian Affairs, 18th and C Streets NW, Washington DC 20245, (202) 208-4871.

United Negro College Fund

Nearly everyone has seen their impressive television commercials. Here's what they do: With funds received from individual and corporate dollars all over the U.S., the Fund awards thousands of scholarships each year to students attending one of the forty-two affiliated colleges and universities—all predominantly black, all in the South (if we count southern Ohio).

More than $5 million each year is awarded in scholarships, some administered by the individual schools and some by the Fund itself. Applicants must be high school students or graduates with a good record, and a good score on the Scholastic Aptitude Test. Further information and a list of participating schools are available from the United Negro College Fund, 500 East 62nd Street, New York NY 10021, (212) 326-1100.

Here are some other resources:

American Indian Science and Engineering Society, Scholarship Coordinator, 1630 30th Street, Suite 301, Boulder, CO 80301-1014

Scholarships totaling $400,000 to 250 American Indian undergraduate or graduate students in engineering, health sciences, or business fields.

China Times Cultural Foundation, 43-27 36th Street, Long Island City, NY 11101

Thirty-six grants totaling $95,000 to undergraduate and graduate students of Chinese ancestry, and to scholars specializing in Chinese studies.

CSU Forgivable Loan/Doctoral Incentive Program

See listing under Resources for Students with Disabilities

Charles and Nancy Oden Luce Trust, c/o Financial Aid Office, Umatilla Indian Reservation, Pendleton, OR 97801

Five grants totaling $11,055 for members of the federated tribes of the Umatilla Indian Reservation to obtain a liberal arts, professional, or vocational education.

Jackie Robinson Foundation, Inc., Three West 35th Street, New York, NY 10001-2204

More than $300,000 to provide four-year college scholarships for minority youth with financial need.

Society of Hispanic Professional Engineers Foundation, 5400 East Olympic Boulevard, Suite 210, Los Angeles, CA 90022

Scholarships totaling $200,000 to 250 Hispanic American students seeking careers in engineering and science.

Swiss Benevolent Society of Chicago, 6440 North Bosworth Avenue, Chicago, IL 60626

Thirty-nine grants totaling $46,826 for undergraduate students of Swiss descent residing in Illinois or southern Wisconsin.

United Negro College Fund Scholarships

Applications are available from any UNCF university.

Over 1,500 awards totaling $3.4 million to students attending UNCF institutions.

Scholarships Linked to Religious Membership or Background

While many local, regional, and national church organizations offer scholarship money, most programs are in the amounts of fifty to several hundred dollars, and/or are extremely regional in scope ("$50 to Baptists living in Tuscaloosa, Alabama"). Following are some of the more substantial ones.

Baptist

Baptist Life Association, Scholarship Committee, 8555 Main Street, Buffalo, NY 14221.

$1,000 a year for up to seven years to people insured by the Association.

Charles B. Keese Educational Fund, P.O. Box 3748, Martinsville, VA 24115.

More than 900 loans or grants per year, $1,000 average, for residents of Virginia or North Carolina, attending Southern Baptist schools.

Catholic

Knights of Columbus, Director of Scholarship Aid, P.O. Box 1670, New Haven, CT 06507.

Twelve scholarships for children of members, to attend Catholic colleges. Low-interest loans to members and their families. A separate scholarship fund is available for Canadian members and their families.

Christian (nondenominational)

Bertha Lambert Memorial Fund, Inc., 725 Lincolnshire Lane, Findlay, OH 45840.

Grants totaling $17,041 to individuals training for Christian service.

Precious Moments Foundation, 480 Chapel Road, Carthage, MO 64836.

Nine grants totaling $27,235 to Christian students, especially those from the Philippines.

Islamic

The Cultural Society, Inc., 200 West 19th Street, Panama City, FL 32405.

Scholarships for Muslim students.

Jewish

Council of Jewish Federations, 575 Lexington Avenue, New York, NY 10022.

Up to $7,000 a year for Jewish college seniors or graduate students who will later work for the Jewish Federations.

Hebrew Free Loan Society, 205 East 42nd Street, New York, NY 10017 and 703 Market Street, San Francisco, CA 94103.

No-interest short-term loans for students (up to $750, up to ten months). Nearly a million borrowers in over ninety years of service.

Jewish Vocational Service, 6715 Minnetonka Boulevard, St. Louis Park, MN 55426.

$2,500 a year for juniors, seniors, or graduate students in certain fields including Jewish education, social work, and the rabbinate. Recipients either repay the amount at low interest or work for one year in Minneapolis for each year of scholarship awarded.

JWB, 15 East 26th Street, New York, NY 10010.

Grants to college students who are committed to the work of Jewish Community Centers, the YMHA, or the YWHA. Juniors, seniors, and graduate students are eligible.

Loeb Farm School for Jewish Children, Inc., 505 Redondo Drive, Unit 310, Downers Grove, IL 60516.

Seven grants totaling $8,750 for Jewish students studying agriculture in the U.S.

Marcus and Theresa Levie Educational Fund, c/o Jewish Federation of Metropolitan Chicago, One South Franklin Street, Chicago, IL 60606.

Twenty-nine grants totaling $196,000 to Jewish students who reside in Cook County and plan for careers in the helping professions.

Wexner Foundation, 41 South High Street, Suite 3390, Columbus, OH 43215-6190.

Forty-nine grants totaling $247,841 to Jewish individuals pursuing Jewish studies.

Lutheran

Aid Association for Lutherans, Appleton, WI 54919.

Four hundred scholarships per year to high school seniors who are insured by this organization, to attend any college. Two other sets of awards are available for Lutheran nonminority students and for Lutheran minority students attending Lutheran colleges and universities.

Lutheran Brotherhood, Financial Aid Coordinator, 625 Fourth Avenue South, Box 857, Minneapolis, MN 55415.

Over $1.6 million under two scholarship programs: for Lutherans, and for Lutheran Brotherhood members.

Lutheran Church in America, Unified Education Fund, 2900 Queen Lane, Philadelphia, PA 19129.

Scholarship grants to American Indians who are also Lutherans.

Methodist

United Methodist Church, Office of Loans and Scholarships, P.O. Box 871, Nashville, TN 37202.

Low-interest loans of $700 to $1,000 per year to members of the church attending United Methodist colleges.

Presbyterian

Presbyterian Church (USA), 100 Witherspoon Street, Louisville, KY 40202-1396

Over $320,000 to Presbyterian high school seniors who are 1) of a racial minority, or 2) planning to attend a Presbyterian-affiliated institution.

United Presbyterian Church, Office of Financial Aid for Studies, 475 Riverside Drive, Room 430, New York, NY 10115.

One hundred fifty scholarships of up to $1,400 per year for communicant members of the church attending certain affiliated schools. Also twenty-five $500 scholarships are based on a competitive essay contest. Additional scholarships for minority incoming freshmen who are church members.

Quaker

United Society of Friends Women Trust, R.R. 1, Box 550, Camby, IN 46113.

Fifty grants totaling $34,038 for members of the United Society of Friends, primarily for seminary study.

Reformed Church

Reformed Church in America, Office of Human Resources, 475 Riverside Drive, New York, NY 10115.

Several programs offering low-interest loans or grants to church members. Some are for minorities; some are for study at specific schools; some are for students preparing for church-related careers.

Other

The Roothbert Fund, Inc., 475 Riverside Drive, Room 252, New York, NY 10115.

> *Ninety-two grants totaling $115,411 for students with strong spiritual values considering a career in teaching.*

Scholarships with Geographical Strings Attached

These listings do not include those (a great number) with very narrow geographical restrictions such as "residents of the Lake Amanor region of Plumas County, California" or "graduates of Benson High School in Chicago."

Western Region

Viola Vestal Coulter Foundation, Inc., c/o Norwest Bank, N.A., 1740 Broadway, Denver, CO 80274-8681

> *Scholarships totaling $129,500 for undergraduate and graduate students at designated colleges in the western U.S.*

Midwestern Region

The Bush Foundation, East 900 First National Bank Building, 332 Minnesota Street, St. Paul, MN 55101

> *Grants totaling $529,575 to residents of Minnesota, North Dakota , and South Dakota, for career advancement.*

Dora L. Mahanay Educational Trust, P.O. Box 27, Jefferson, IA 50129-0027

> *Loans totaling $69,663 to residents of Iowa and Nebraska.*

Edward Arthur Mellinger Educational Foundation, Inc., 1025 East Broadway, Monmouth, IL 61462

> *Almost $1 million in grants and loans to over 1,000 graduate and undergraduate students residing or studying in western Illinois and eastern Iowa.*

New England Region

Marjorie Sells Carter Boy Scout Scholarship Fund, P.O. Box 527, West Chatham, MA 02669

> *Ninety-four college scholarships totaling $120,500 to former Boy Scouts who are residents of New England.*

Northeastern Region

Ernestine Matthews Trust, P.O Box 10367, Rockville, MD 20849

Forty-six grants totaling $53,000 to applicants from Washington DC, Maryland, Pennsylvania, Virginia, and West Virginia, based upon financial need.

Lalitta Nash McKaig Foundation, c/o PNC Bank, N.A., Trust Dept. 944, One Oliver Plaza, 27th Floor, Pittsburgh, PA 15265-0970

Grants totaling $313,423 to residents of certain counties in Pennsylvania, West Virginia, and Maryland.

Otto Sussman Trust, P.O. Box 1374, Trainsmeadow Station, Flushing, NY 11370

Grants totaling $211,850 to residents of New York, New Jersey, and Pennsylvania who are in need due to tragic or unusual circumstances.

Southeastern Region

Pickett and Hatcher Educational Fund, Inc., P.O. Box 8169, Columbus, GA 31908

Over $1.6 million in student loans to undergraduates residing in the southeastern U.S., to be used for liberal arts education.

Alabama

A. H. Bean Foundation, c/o First Alabama Bank Trust Department, 2222 Ninth Street, Tuscaloosa, AL 35401

Scholarships totaling $112,716 to Christian Alabama residents who are active members of a church.

David R. Dunlap, Jr. Memorial Trust, c/o First Alabama Bank, P.O. Drawer 2527, Mobile, AL 36622

Student loans totaling $153,805 to residents of Mobile and Baldwin counties, AL.

Joanna F. Reed Medical Scholarship Trust, c/o First National Bank, P.O. Box 469, Brewton, AL 36427-0469

Six grants of $7,500 each to medical students residing in Alabama or northwest Florida.

The Simpson Foundation, c/o First Alabama Bank, P.O. Box 511, Montgomery, AL 36134

Awards twenty scholarships totaling $323,500 to residents of Wilcox County, Alabama.

Alaska

CIRI Foundation, P.O. Box 93330, Anchorage, AK 99509-3330
Scholarships totaling $223,527 for Alaska Natives of Cook Inlet Region (Eskimo, Indian, and Aleut).

Huna Totem Heritage Foundation, 9309 Glacier Highway, Suite A-103, Juneau, AK 99801
Twelve grants totaling $18,273 available to shareholders of the Huna Totem and their descendants.

Arizona

B & L Educational Foundation, 2111 Northridge Drive, NE, Grand Rapids, MI 49505
Fifty-nine grants totaling $53,050, to students residing or attending school in either Arizona or Michigan.

BF Foundation, 23 East Fine Avenue, Flagstaff, AZ 86001-3217
Offers grants totaling $248,000 through school financial aid offices, for undergraduates who are Arizona residents.

Father Joseph Patterson Foundation, Inc., 2342 West Emelita Avenue, Mesa, AZ 85202
Thirty-eight grants totaling $35,000 to residents of Arizona.

Seed Money for Growth Foundation, Inc., 4716 North Dromedary Road, Phoenix, AZ 85018-2939
Forty-six grants totaling $44,406 for a variety of purposes, to Arizona residents only.

Benjamin J. Webber Scholarship Fund/Josephine M. Webber Scholarship Fund, Webber Educational Grants Committee, Arizona Association of Family and Consumer Services, 4861 North Via Serenidad, Tucson, AZ 85718-5715
Seven scholarships totaling $59,520 in home economics and nutrition, for Mexican-American bilingual females from mining towns in Arizona.

Arkansas

Arkansas Community Foundation, Inc., 700 South Rock, Little Rock, AR 72202
Scholarships and loans totaling $110,628 for Arkansas residents.

Jesse W. Cannon Scholarship Foundation, 112 South East Avenue, Fayetteville, AR 72701
Loans totaling $32,900 to students attending the University of Arkansas.

The Murphy Foundation, Union Building, El Dorado, AR 71730
Thirty scholarships totaling $57,804 to residents of southern Arkansas.

Godfrey Thomas Foundation, Inc., 623 South Tyler, De Witt, AR 72042
Awards scholarships totaling $60,675 to De Witt, Arkansas residents.

Trinity Foundation, P.O. Box 7008, Pine Bluff, AR 71611-7008
Scholarships totaling $61,689 to students graduating from certain high schools in Pine Bluff, Little Rock, Benton, and Bauxite, AR.

California

Bank of America—Giannini Foundation, Bank of America Center, Department 3246, Box 37000, San Francisco, CA 94137
Twelve grants of $25,000 each for postdoctoral research at medical schools in California.

California Masonic Foundation, 1111 California Street, San Francisco, CA 94108-2284
Scholarships totaling $187,750 to California undergraduates who are U.S. citizens.

Ebell of Los Angeles Scholarship Endowment Fund, 743 South Lucerne Boulevard, Los Angeles, CA 90005
Grants totaling $144,510 to students who reside and attend college in Los Angeles County.

William and Marian Ghidotti Foundation, 3961 Desabia Road, Cameron Park, CA 95682
Over $227,000 in scholarships to residents of Nevada County, CA.

Leon L. Granoff Foundation, P.O. Box 2148, Gardena, CA 90247-0148
Fourteen grants totaling $135,621 to California residents in undergraduate programs in California.

Jessie Klicka Foundation, Wells Fargo Trust Department, 101 West Broadway, Suite 400, San Diego, CA 92101
Thirty-five grants totaling $48,500 to graduates of San Diego County schools.

Koomruian Education Fund, c/o Bank of America, 333 South Beaudry Avenue, Box 16, Los Angeles, CA 90017-1466
Grants totaling $28,477 to California residents of Armenian descent.

Peninsula Community Foundation, 1700 South El Camino Real, #300, San Mateo, CA 94402-3049
Grants totaling $99,735 to residents of San Mateo County and northern Santa Clara County, CA.

The Mabel Wilson Richards Scholarship Fund, 5301 Laurel Canyon Boulevard, #233, North Hollywood, CA 91607-2736

Grants totaling $373,200 for females residing in Los Angeles or certain other California communities, and attending certain California colleges.

Sacramento Regional Foundation, 1610 Arden Way, Suite 298, Sacramento, CA 95815

Twenty grants totaling $34,800 for residents of Sacramento, Yolo, Placer, and El Dorado Counties, CA.

Santa Barbara Foundation, 15 East Carillo Street, Santa Barbara, CA 93101-2780

Over $1.4 million in student loans to residents of Santa Barbara County.

Scaife Scholarship Foundation, 1547 Lakeside Drive, Oakland, CA 94612

Sixty-six grants totaling $222,250 to male graduates of Northern California public schools, whose parents were born in the U.S.

Mary Ellen Warner Educational Trust, 10371 Rochester Avenue, Los Angeles, CA 90024

Sixteen loans totaling $87,250 to upper division and graduate students who are permanent California residents and are attending California institutions.

Colorado

Boettcher Foundation, 600 17th Street, Suite 2210 South, Denver, CO 80202

Scholarships totaling more than $1.3 million, to Colorado residents.

Colorado Masons Benevolent Fund Association, 7955 East Arapahoe Court, Suite 1200, Englewood, CO 80112-1362

Grants totaling $273,450 to graduates of Colorado high schools, for higher education in the state.

Sachs Foundation, 90 South Cascade Avenue, Suite 1410, Colorado Springs, CO 80903

Grants totaling $611,043 to 257 African American Colorado residents.

E. Isabella Stupfel Trust, 505 Eisenhower Drive, Louisville, CO 80022

Fifteen grants totaling $22,465 to Colorado residents.

The Thatcher Foundation, Minnequa Bank of Pueblo, Pueblo, CO 81004

Twenty-three grants totaling $44,000 to undergraduate residents of Pueblo County, CO.

Connecticut

William H. Chapman Foundation, P.O. Box 1321, New London, CT 06320
Grants totaling $69,727 to undergraduate residents of New London County, CT.

Jacob L. and Lewis Fox Foundation Trust, 31 Knollwood Road, Farmington, CT 06032
Scholarships totaling $123,844 for graduates of Hartford, CT public schools.

The MacCundy-Salisbury Educational Foundation, Inc., Nine Mansewood Road, Old Lyme, CT 06371
Seventy-four grants totaling $122,000 to residents of Lyme and Old Lyme, CT.

The Mirza Mehdi Charitable Trust, c/o Lee and Young, P.C., Ten High Street, Boston, MA 02110-1605
Grants totaling $6,555, especially for Connecticut residents to attend the University of Connecticut.

The Meriden Foundation, c/o Meriden Trust and Safe Deposit Co., P.O. Box 951, Meriden, CT 06450
Seventy-one grants totaling $84,325 primarily to residents of the Meriden-Wallingford, CT area.

James Z. Naurison Scholarship Fund: see Massachusetts.

Woman's Seamen's Friend Society of Connecticut, 42 Forbes Avenue, New Haven, CT 06512
Grants for the study of marine sciences at a Connecticut institution, or for Connecticut residents to study marine sciences out-of-state.

Delaware

George E. Gordy Family Educational Trust Fund, c/o Wilmington Trust Co., 1100 North Market Street, Wilmington, DE 19890-0001
Thirty-two grants totaling $78,177 to needy graduates of Sussex County, DE high schools.

John B. Lynch Scholarship Foundation, P.O. Box 4248, Wilmington, DE 19807
Grants totaling $148,989 to undergraduate residents of the Wilmington, DE area.

Joseph P. Pyle Trust, c/o PNC Bank, 222 Delaware Avenue, 16th Floor, Wilmington, DE 19899
One grant of $21,540 to a Wilmington, DE resident, between seventeen and twenty-one years of age, entering the first year of college.

Florida

Ebba Alm Educational Fund, c/o SunBank of Tampa Bay, 825 Broadway, Dunedin, FL 34698
Ten grants totaling $19,000 to needy male residents of Florida.

The Community Foundation for Palm Beach and Martin Counties, 324 Datura Street, Suite 340, West Palm Beach, FL 33401-5431
Fifty-four grants totaling $74,458 to residents of Palm Beach and Martin Counties, FL.

Fort Pierce Memorial Hospital Scholarship Foundation, c/o Lawnwood Medical Center, P.O. Box 188, 1700 South 23rd Street, Fort Pierce, FL 34950
Twenty-four grants totaling $180,880 to residents of St. Lucie County, FL who are studying for a career in the health field.

Gore Family Memorial Foundation, 4747 North Ocean Drive, #204, Fort Lauderdale, FL 33302
Grants totaling $112,993 to residents of Broward County, FL and to handicapped students from anywhere in the U.S.

Nina Haven Charitable Foundation, c/o Guidance Office, Marlin County High School, 2801 South Kanner Highway, Stuart, FL 34994
Eighty-five grants totaling $94,475 to graduates of Marlin County high schools and local community colleges.

Joanna F. Reed Medical Scholarship Trust: see Alabama.

Richardson Foundation Inc., Washington Trust Building, Room 418, Washington, PA 15301
Grants totaling $229,901 to residents of Indian River, FL.

Rinker Companies Foundation Inc., 1501 Belvedere Road, West Palm Beach, FL 33406
Seventy grants totaling $104,270 to Florida residents with business or construction industry-related majors.

Grace Margaret Watterson Trust, c/o First Union National Bank of Florida, P.O. Drawer 2720, Daytona Beach, FL 32115
Grants totaling $93,475 to graduates of high schools in Daytona Beach and Ormond Beach, FL.

J.J. Wiggins Memorial Trust, P.O. Box 1111, Moore Haven, FL 33471
Grants totaling $126,065 to residents of Glades County, FL.

Georgia

Fuller E. Callaway Foundation, P.O. Box 790, 209 Broome Street, La Grange, GA 30241
Eighty-six scholarships totaling $260,348 to residents of Troup County, GA.

Church Homes Foundation Inc., 706 West Conway Drive, NW, Atlanta, GA 30302
Sixty-six scholarships totaling $73,450 to residents of metropolitan Atlanta, GA.

Ty Cobb Educational Fund, P.O. Box 725, Forest Park, GA 30051
Sixty-seven grants totaling $225,333 to needy Georgia residents who have completed one year of college.

William F. Cooper Scholarship Trust, c/o FUNB-CMG, P.O. Box 9947, Savannah, GA 31412
Seventy-eight grants totaling $41,784 to female residents of Chatham County, GA.

Allan C. and Lelia J. Garden Foundation, P.O. Box 308, Fitzgerald, GA 31750
Loans and grants totaling $123,882 to students in Macon, GA.

Harold Hirsch Scholarship Fund, c/o Kilpatrick & Cody, 100 Peachtree Street NW, Suite 3100, Atlanta, GA 30303
Grants totaling $55,400 to Atlanta, Georgia residents.

Student Aid Foundation, 1393 Sheffield Parkway, Marietta, GA 30062
Sixty-one low-interest loans totaling $149,593 to female residents of Georgia.

Hawaii

Educational Fund of the Honolulu Branch of the American Association of University Women, 1802 Keeaumoku Street, Honolulu, HI 96822
Twelve grants totaling $20,000 to female residents of Hawaii for graduate and undergraduate study.

Chung Kun Ai Foundation, P.O. Box 1559, Honolulu, HI 96806
Seven grants totaling $12,000 to needy residents of Hawaii.

Fukunaga Scholarship Foundation, Scholarship Selection Committee, P.O. Box 2788, Honolulu, HI 96803
Forty-five grants totaling $84,750 to residents of Hawaii studying business administration.

The Hawaii Community Foundation, 222 Merchant Street, Honolulu, HI 96813

Grants totaling over $1.3 million to residents of Hawaii.

Gertrude S. Straub Trust Estate, c/o Hawaii Community Foundation, 222 Merchant Street, Honolulu, HI 96813

Grants totaling $203,435 to Hawaii public high school graduates to attend mainland U.S. colleges for the study of subjects relating to the promotion of international peace.

Hans and Clara Davis Zimmerman Foundation, c/o Hawaii Community Foundation, 222 Merchant Street, Honolulu, HI 96813

Grants totaling $363,240 to Hawaii residents pursuing studies leading to a career in the health fields.

Illinois

The Aurora Foundation, 111 West Downer Place, Suite 312, Aurora, IL 60506-5136

Scholarships and loans totaling $129,575 to students residing in or near Aurora, IL.

Davey Scholarship Foundation, c/o Bank One, Springfield, East Old State Capitol Plaza, Springfield, IL 62701

Forty-eight grants totaling $106,109 to high school graduates of Sangamon, Morgan, and Christian Counties, IL.

Flora S. McCourtney Trust, c/o Boatmen's Trust Co., 100 North Broadway, P.O. Box 14737, St. Louis, MO 63178

Grants totaling $226,000 to high school graduates in Sangamon County, IL.

Herbert T. McLean Memorial Fund, 503 West Miller Street, Bloomington, IL 61701

Twenty-four grants totaling $22,750 to residents of Illinois.

A. Franklin Pilcharo Foundation, c/o M.P.E. and G., 1661 Feehanville Drive, Suite 301, Mt. Prospect, IL 60016

Grants totaling $71,213 to students attending educational institutions in Illinois.

Robin Scholarship Foundation, 1333 North Wells Street, Chicago, IL 60610

Grants totaling $136,090 to promising Illinois high school seniors from low-income families.

Harry L. and John L. Smysor Memorial Fund, c/o First Mid-Illinois Bank & Trust, 1515 Charleston Avenue, Mattoon, IL 61938-3932
Grants totaling $186,205 to local high school students for higher education.

Indiana

Olive B. Cole Foundation Inc., 3242 Mallard Cove Lane, Fort Wayne, IN 46804
Grants totaling $143,296 to residents of Noble County, Indiana and graduates of its high schools.

Mary Frances Hernandez and Roy E. Smith Scholarship Fund, c/o First Citizens Bank, N.A., P.O. Box 1125, Michigan City, IN 46360
Twenty grants totaling $49,323 to residents of the Michigan City, Indiana area.

The Elizabeth A. Mahnken Foundation Inc., 12210 North Mariposa Drive, Syracuse, IN 46567
Ten grants totaling $44,021 to Indiana undergraduates attending state-supported institutions.

McDonald Memorial Fund Trust, c/o First National Bank of Warsaw, P.O. Box 1447, Warsaw, IN 46581
Loans totaling $131,350 to Koscuisko County, Indiana residents.

Greater Seymour Trust Fund, P.O. Box 1001, Seymour, IN 47274
Fifty-four grants totaling $69,000 to residents of Jackson County, IN.

Oliver Storer Scholarship Foundation, c/o Beasley, Glickison, Retherford, and Buckles, 110 East Charles Street, Muncie, IN 47305
Forty-three grants totaling $119,488 to graduating seniors of Delaware County, IN.

Charles and Ada Williams Memorial Scholarship Fund, Inc., West Washington High School, Campbellsburg, IN 47167
Sixteen grants totaling $11,250 to students attending Indiana colleges and universities.

Iowa

Fahrney Education Foundation, c/o Firstar Bank, Trust Department, 123 East Third Street, Ottumwa, IA 52501
Ninety-seven grants totaling $135,712 to residents of Wapello County, Iowa to attend Iowa colleges and universities.

George S. and Grace A. Jay Memorial Trust, P.O. Box 57, 612½ West Sheridan Avenue, Shenandoah, IA 51601

Loans totaling $108,800 to graduates of Shenandoah, Essex, and Farragut, Iowa high schools.

Lee Endowment Foundation, Muse Scholarship Fund, 500 College Drive, Mason City, IA 50401

Grants totaling $113,512 primarily, but not exclusively, to residents of Mason City and Cerro Gordo County, Iowa.

Mabel E. Sherman Educational Fund, c/o Citizens First National Bank, East Fifth and Lake, Storm Lake, IA 50588

Loans totaling $66,544 to Iowa residents, with preference given to residents of Ida and Cherokee counties.

Straub Foundation, 7306 Oliver Smith Drive, Des Moines, IA 50322

Thirty-seven grants totaling $22,044 to residents of Iowa.

Kansas

Jennie G. and Pearl Abell Education Trust, 717 Main Street, P.O. Box 487, Ashland, KS 67831

Sixty-seven grants totaling $136,629 to graduates of Clark County, Kansas high schools, or current Clark County residents.

Dane G. Hansen Foundation, P.O. Box 187, Logan, KS 67646

Grants totaling $193,750 to graduates of high schools in northwest Kansas.

Walter S. and Evan C. Jones Foundation, 527 Commercial Street, Room 515, Emporia, KS 66801

Grants totaling $158,367 to residents of Lyon, Coffey, or Osage Counties, KS.

Lloyd E. and Katherine S. Winslow Education Trust, Superintendent of Schools, P.O. Box 35, Moran, KS 66755

One hundred grants totaling $64,750 to residents of Moran, Marmaton Township, and Allen County, Kansas for higher education.

Kentucky

John T. and Ada Diederich Educational Trust Fund, c/o National City Bank, Trust Dept., P.O. Box 1270, Ashland, KY 41105-1270

Forty-eight grants totaling $344,800 to residents of Boyd, Greenup, Martin, Lawrence, and Carter counties, Kentucky.

Blanche and Thomas Hope Memorial Fund, c/o National City Bank, P.O. Box 1270, Ashland, KY 41105-1270

Seventy grants totaling $130,300 to students graduating from high schools in Boyd and Greenup counties, Kentucky.

Kincaid Foundation Inc., Central Bank and Trust Co., 510 Kincaid Towers, Lexington, KY 40507

Thirty grants totaling $48,000 to graduates of Fayette County, Kentucky high schools.

The Louisville Community Foundation Inc., Waterfront Plaza Building, 325 West Main Street, Suite 1110, Louisville, KY 40202

Grants totaling $135,224 to students in the greater Louisville, Kentucky area.

James W. Willmott Memorial Trust, 301 East Main Street, Lexington, KY 40507

Sixty-five grants totaling $34,150 to residents of Bourbon County, KY and adjacent counties.

John B. and Brownie Young Memorial Fund, Owensboro National Bank, Trust Department, 230 Frederica Street, Owensboro, KY 42301

Fifty-eight grants totaling $223,300 to students in Owensboro, Davies, and McClean counties, Kentucky.

Louisiana

Barnabas Ministries of Shreveport, 4451 Charter Point Boulevard, Jacksonville, FL 32211

Six grants totaling $16,449 to worthy students in Louisiana.

The William T. and Ethel Lewis Burton Foundation, One Lakeshore Drive, Suite 1700, Lake Charles, LA 70629

Grants totaling $219,103 to high school seniors in southwest Louisiana.

Ed E. and Gladys Hurley Foundation, c/o Premier Bank, N.A., Trust Dept., P.O. Box 21116, Shreveport, LA 71154

Loans totaling $81,000 to residents of Louisiana and Texas to attend the institution of their choice.

Agnes T. Maguire Trust, c/o Premier Bank, N.A., Trust Dept., P.O. Box 91210, Baton Rouge, LA 70821-9210

Fifty-five loans totaling $98,500 to female residents of Louisiana.

ⁱasonic Educational Foundation Inc., 1300 Masonic Temple Building, ᶜt. Charles Avenue, New Orleans, LA 70130

ᵗs totaling $17,802 to Louisiana residents.

Willis and Mildred Pellerin Foundation, c/o A.A. Harman and Co., P.O. Box 400, Kenner, LA 70063

Grants totaling $65,000 to Louisiana residents at Louisiana colleges and universities.

Fred B. and Ruth B. Zigler Foundation, P.O. Box 986, Jennings, LA 70546-0986

Grants totaling $132,434 to graduating seniors of Jefferson Davis Parish, Louisiana high schools.

Maine

Herbert E. and Marion K. Bragg Foundation, Crestar Bank, 510 South Jefferson Street, Roanoke, VA 24011

Twenty-nine grants totaling $63,000 to students at institutions in Virginia and Maine, with preference for students from Maine.

The Maine Community Foundation Inc., 210 Main Street, P.O. Box 148, Ellsworth, ME 04605

Grants totaling $156,700 to Maine residents.

Pinkham Family Charitable Trust, Casco Northern Bank, Trust Dept., P.O. Box 1029, Presque Isle, ME 04769-1029

Thirty-eight grants totaling $30,472 to residents of Aroostook County, ME.

Clyde Russell Scholarship Fund, P.O. Box 2457, Augusta, ME 04338

Three grants of $10,000 each to legal residents of Maine.

Helen F. Wylie Foundation, 417 Main Street, P.O. Box 2, Rockland, ME 04841

Twenty-five grants totaling $26,377 to students residing in Owls Head, ME.

Maryland

Loats Foundation Inc., c/o Evangelical Lutheran Church, 35 East Church Street, Frederick, MD 21701

Thirty-eight grants totaling $31,050 to needy residents of Frederick County, MD.

J.C. Stewart Memorial Trust, 7718 Finns Lane, Lanham, MD 20706

Grants and loans totaling $254,000 to Maryland residents.

Columbus W. Thorn Jr. Foundation, 109 East Main Street, Elkton, MD 21921

Loans totaling $254,200 to needy residents of Cecil County, MD.

Florence B. Trueman Educational Trust, P.O. Box 909, Main Street, Prince Frederick, MD 20678

Forty-four grants totaling $50,300 to graduates of public high schools in Calvert County, MD.

Massachusetts

Lou and Lucienne Brightman Scholarship Foundation, c/o Eastern Bank and Trust Co., 94 Pleasant Street, Malden, MA 02148

Twenty grants totaling $15,350 to Massachusetts residents.

The James W. Colgan Loan Fund, c/o Fleet Bank of Massachusetts, N.A., P.O. Box 9003, Springfield, MA 01101

Loans totaling $382,473 to those who have resided in Massachusetts for at least five years.

Edwards Scholarship Fund, 10 Post Office Square South, Suite 1230, Boston, MA 02109

Loans totaling $245,700 to residents of Boston, MA.

James Z. Naurison Scholarship Fund, c/o Fleet Bank of Massachusetts, N.A., P.O. Box 9006, Springfield, MA 01102-9006

Grants totaling $366,027 to residents of certain counties in Massachusetts and Connecticut.

Francis Ouimet Scholarship Fund, Scholarship Director, 190 Park Road, Weston, MA 02193-3401

Scholarships totaling $370,000 to 250 students "who have given three years service to golf in Massachusetts as a caddie, bag room/pro shop attendant, or grounds crew worker."

Horace Smith Fund, c/o Fleet Trust Co., 1459 Main Street, Box 3034, Springfield, MA 01101

Grants and loans totaling $714,958 to residents and high school graduates of Hampden County, MA.

Albert H. and Reuben S. Stone Fund, 232 Sherman Street, Gardner, MA 01440

Grants totaling $171,450 to residents of Gardner, MA.

Sudbury Foundation, 278 Old Sudbury Road, Sudbury, MA 01776

Scholarships and loans totaling $378,150 to residents of Sudbury, MA.

Urann Foundation, P.O. Box 1788, Brockton, MA 02403

Scholarships to members of Massachusetts families engaged in the
·oduction of cranberries.

Worcester Community Foundation Inc., 44 Front Street, Suite
·ster, MA 01608-1782

·ling $149,465 to residents of Worcester County, MA.

Michigan

B & L Educational Foundation: see Arizona.

C.K. Eddy Family Memorial Fund, 101 North Washington Avenue, Saginaw, MI 48607

Loans totaling $389,000 to residents of Saginaw County, MI.

H. T. Ewald Foundation, 15175 East Jefferson Avenue, Grosse Pointe, MI 48230

Thirty grants totaling $72,706 to high school seniors in the Detroit area.

The Grand Rapids Foundation, 209-C Waters Building, 161 Ottawa, NW, Grand Rapids, MI 49503-2703

Grants totaling $146,522 to Kent County, Michigan residents.

Michael Jeffers Memorial Fund, Second National Bank of Saginaw, 101 North Washington Avenue, Saginaw, MI 48607

Loans totaling $313,110 to Saginaw County, Michigan residents.

Midland Foundation, 812 West Main Street, P.O. Box 289, Midland, MI 48640

Loans and scholarships totaling $90,580 to residents of the Midland County, Michigan area for tuition, books, and fees only.

Muskegon County Community Foundation Inc., Community Foundation Building, Suite 304, 425 West Western Avenue, Muskegon, MI 49440

Grants totaling $190,655 to students in Muskegon County, MI.

Winship Memorial Scholarship Foundation, c/o Commercial Bank— Battle Creek, Trust Division, 25 West Michigan Avenue, Battle Creek, MI 49017

Eighty-six grants totaling $106,960 to graduates of Battle Creek, Michigan area public high schools.

Minnesota

Marshall H. and Nellie Alworth Memorial Fund, 506 Alworth Building, Duluth, MN 55802

Grants totaling almost $1 million to residents of northeastern Minnesota who are studying the sciences.

The Blandin Foundation, 100 Pokegama Avenue North, Grand Rapids, MN 55744

Grants totaling $417,268 to recent graduates of an Itasca County, Hill City, or Remer, Minnesota high school.

Minnesota Foundation, 600 Norwest Center, St. Paul, MN 55101

Three grants of $1,000 each to Minnesota residents.

The Saint Paul Foundation, 600 Norwest Center, St. Paul, MN 55101-1797

Scholarships totaling $178,864 to residents of St. Paul and Minneapolis, MN.

Harlan R. Thurston Foundation, 832 Eastwood Lane, Anoka, MN 55303

Student loans totaling $365,053 to graduates of Anoka-Hennepin Independent School District, MN.

Tozer Foundation Inc., c/o First Trust, N.A., First National Bank Building, P.O. Box 64704, St. Paul, MN 55164-0704

Grants totaling $521,700 to graduating high school students in Pine, Kanabec, and Washington counties, MN.

Whiteside Scholarship Fund Trust, Room 210, Central Administration Building, Lake Avenue and Second Street, Duluth, MN 55802

Sixty-two grants totaling $206,800 to graduates of Duluth, Minnesota high schools who are in the top 10 percent of their class.

Mississippi

D. A. Biglane Foundation, 75 Melrose-Montebello Parkway, Natchez, MS 39120

Seven grants totaling $39,820 to residents of the Natchez, Mississippi area.

Carl and Virginia Johnson Day Trust, 108 West Madison, Yazoo City, MS 39194

Interest-free student loans totaling $207,650 to Mississippi residents attending Mississippi schools.

Feild Co-Operative Association Inc., P.O. Box 5054, Jackson, MS 39296-5054

Educational loans to Mississippi residents.

Charles E. Platner Charitable Trust, Financial Aid Director, Delta State University, Cleveland, MS 38733

Ten grants totaling $31,701 to residents of the Skene Consolidated School District, MS.

Missouri

James H. Fullbright and Monroe L. Swyers Foundation, c/o Boatmen's Trust Company, 100 North Broadway, P.O. Box 14737, St. Louis, MO 63178

Eighty-one grants totaling $179,500 to Missouri residents.

May H. Ilgenfritz Testamentary Trust, 108 West Pacific, Sedalia, MO 65301

Grants totaling $164,325 to high school students in the Sedalia, Missouri area.

Joe Ingram Trust "B" Comm., 111 West Third Street, Salisbury, MO 65281
Loans totaling $568,038 to residents of the Chariton County, Missouri area, for undergraduate and vocational education.

MFA Foundation, MFA Auditing Department, 615 Locust Street, Columbia, MO 65201
Grants totaling $243,954 to high school seniors residing in MFA Oil Co. areas of operation.

Edward F. Swinney Student Loan Fund, c/o Boatmen's First National Bank of Kansas City, 14 West Tenth Street, Kansas City, MO 64105
Thirty-seven loans totaling $75,000 to Missouri residents attending colleges in Missouri.

James L. and Nellie M. Westlake Scholarship Fund, 111 South Bemiston, Suite 412, Clayton, MO 63105
Grants totaling $576,905 to high school seniors residing in Missouri.

Montana

Charles M. Bair Memorial Trust, First Trust Company of Montana, P.O. Box 30678, Billings, MT 59115
Thirty grants totaling $130,539 to graduates of certain Montana high schools.

Dodd and Dorothy Bryan Foundation: see Wyoming.

Olive Rice Reierson Foundation, c/o Northwest Capital Management, P.O. Box 597, Helena, MT 59624
Sixteen grants totaling $55,000 to graduates of Powell County, Montana high schools.

Nebraska

Weller Foundation Inc., East Highway 20, P.O. Box 636, Atkinson, NE 68713
Grants totaling $188,681 to 215 Nebraska residents to attend vocational education institutions.

Nevada

Russell and Edna Knapp Foundation Trust, c/o First Interstate Bank of Nevada, P.O. Box 30100, Reno, NV 89520-0010
Grants totaling $45,583 to residents of Elko County, NV.

New Hampshire

The Barker Foundation Inc., P.O. Box 328, Nashua, NH 03061
Grants totaling $27,648 to New Hampshire residents.

Abraham Burtman Charity Trust, Burns Building, P.O. Box 608, Dover, NH 03820-4103
Thirty-three grants of $1,000 each to New Hampshire residents.

Henry C. Lord Scholarship Fund Trust, c/o First NH Investment Services, P.O. Box 1017, Concord, NH 03302-1017
Grants totaling $414,684 to needy residents of Peterborough, New Hampshire and contiguous towns.

The New Hampshire Charitable Foundation, 37 Pleasant Street, Concord, NH 03301-4005
Loans totaling $320,849 to New Hampshire residents.

Jason C. Somerville Trust, P.O. Box 299, Bethlehem, NH 03574-0299
Thirty-four grants totaling $50,000 to residents of the Bethlehem, New Hampshire area.

New Jersey

Geraldine R. Dodge Foundation Inc., 163 Madison Avenue, 6th Floor, P.O. Box 1239, Morristown, NJ 07962-1239
Sixty-five grants of $5,000 each to New Jersey teachers and principals, for professional development.

The William Limmer Scholarship Foundation, c/o Hunziker, Merrey, and Jones, 125 Ellison Street, Suite 400, Paterson, NJ 07505
Twenty-eight grants totaling $41,714 to Passaic, New Jersey area residents.

William A. and Mary A. Shreve Foundation, Inc., P.O. Box I, 25 Abe Voorhees Drive, Manasquan, NJ 08736
Twenty-two grants totaling $68,190, primarily for students in New Jersey.

Alfred J. Speak Foundation, c/o Trust Officer, First Fidelity Bank, N.A., 765 Broad Street, Newark, NJ 07102
Twenty-two grants of $1,000 each, to needy young residents of New Jersey.

New Mexico

Carlsbad Foundation Inc., 116 South Canyon Street, Carlsbad, NM 88220
Scholarships and loans to students in the South Eddy County and Carlsbad, New Mexico area.

J. F. Maddox Foundation, P.O. Box 2588, Hobbs, NM 88241-2588
   Thirty-eight loans totaling $37,100 to residents of Lea County, NM.

Viles Foundation Inc., P.O. Box 1177, Las Vegas, NM 87701
   Forty-nine grants totaling $44,450 to needy residents of San Miguel and Mora Counties, NM.

New York

James Gordon Bennett Memorial Corporation, c/o New York Daily News, 220 East 42nd Street, New York, NY 10017
   Ninety-eight grants totaling $106,155 to children of people who have worked on New York City daily newspapers for at least ten years.

M. A. and L. J. Bennett Scholarship Fund, Emerald Society, 677 83rd Street, Brooklyn, NY 11228
   Eighty-seven grants totaling $412,350 to children of New York City police officers.

Chautauqua Region Community Foundation Inc., 104-106 Hotel Jamestown Building, Jamestown, NY 14701
   Over 600 grants totaling $450,000 to residents of Chautauqua, Allegheny, and Cottarangus Counties, NY.

Deo B. Colburn Education Foundation, P.O. Box 824, 15 Saranac Avenue, Lake Placid, NY 12946
   Grants totaling $94,900 to residents of the northern New York State Adirondack region.

Bruce L. Crary Foundation Inc., Hand House, River Street, P.O. Box 396, Elizabethtown, NY 12932
   Over 600 grants totaling $272,120 to residents of five New York counties.

Jewish Foundation for the Education of Women, 330 West 58th Street, 5J, New York, NY 10019
   Grants totaling $848,830 on a non-sectarian basis to 481 women living in the New York metropolitan area.

Lazare and Charlotte Kaplan Foundation Inc., P.O. Box 216, Livingston Manor, NY 12758
   Grants totaling $54,600 to students from Sullivan County, NY.

Alice W. C. Koon Scholastic Fund, c/o Marine Midland Bank, N.A., One Marine Center, 17th Floor, Buffalo, NY 14240
   Thirteen grants totaling $18,425 to undergraduates at New York state universities.

Northern New York Community Foundation Inc., 120 Washington Street, Watertown, NY 13601

Grants totaling $265,486 to residents of Jefferson and Lewis Counties, NY.

The Scholarships Foundation Inc., Canal Street Station, P.O. Box 170, New York, NY 10013

Forty-three grants totaling $60,750 to students over the age of 20, and attending New York institutions.

North Carolina

Iona M. Allen Music Scholarship Fund, c/o Wachovia Bank and Trust Co., N.A., P.O. Box 3099, Winston-Salem, NC 27150

Fifty-two grants totaling $32,525 to high school seniors showing musical talent, and residing in western North Carolina.

Blackwelder Foundation, P.O. Box 1436, Lenoir, NC 28645

Grants to residents of North Carolina, particularly children of hospital workers.

Percy B. Ferebee Endowment, Wachovia Bank of North Carolina, P.O. Box 3099, Winston-Salem, NC 27150

Grants totaling $45,000 to thirty-one residents of certain North Carolina counties to attend North Carolina schools.

Foundation for The Carolinas: see South Carolina.

James G. K. McClure Educational and Development Fund Inc., 11 Sugar Hollow Lane, Fairview, NC 28730

Grants totaling $64,000 to residents of western North Carolina.

North Dakota

Gabriel J. Brown Trust, 112 Avenue E West, Bismarck, ND 58501

Eighty loans totaling $100,000 to North Dakota residents.

Helen Gough Foundation Trust, P.O. Box 156, Stanley, ND 58784

Sixteen grants totaling $11,900 to members of the three affiliated tribes of the Fort Berthold Reservation (Mandon, Hidilsa, Arikara).

C. F. Martell Memorial Foundation, P.O. Box 546, Watford City, ND 58854

Fifty student loans totaling $50,000 to residents of Williams and McKenzie counties, ND.

Ohio

The Hauss-Helms Foundation Inc., c/o Peoples National Bank Building, P.O. Box 25, Wapakoneta, OH 45895

Grants totaling $441,056 to 386 needy graduates of high schools in Auglaize or Allen counties, OH.

John McIntire Educational Fund, c/o First National Bank, Trust Dept., P.O. Box 2668, 422 Main Street, Zanesville, OH 43701

Grants totaling $238,830 to 137 unmarried residents of Zanesville, Ohio who are under the age of twenty-one.

George J. Record School Foundation, P.O. Box 581, Conneaut, OH 44030

Grants totaling $204,404 to eighty-three legal residents of Ashtabula County, OH.

Scholarship Fund, University of Toledo, 2801 West Bancroft Street, Toledo, OH 43606

Grants totaling $23,038 to twenty-one residents of northwest Ohio, and other students at the University of Toledo, OH.

William M. Shinnick Educational Fund, 534 Market Street, Zanesville, OH 43701

Grants and loans totaling $210,941 to residents of Muskingum, OH.

Van Wert County Foundation, 101½ East Main Street, Van Wert, OH 45891

Grants totaling $154,133 to residents of Van Wert County, OH.

Oklahoma

Alfred A. and Tia J. Drummond Foundation, c/o Liberty National Bank and Trust Co., P.O. Box 25848, Trust Dept., Oklahoma City, OK 73125-0848

Fourteen grants totaling $25,000 to students graduating from public high schools in Marshall County, OK.

Laura Fields Trust, P.O. Box 2394, Lawton, OK 73502

Fifty-two student loans totaling $105,576 to residents of Comanche County, OK.

Hyde Foundation, 5108 North Shartel, Oklahoma City, OK 73118-6094

Twenty-one grants totaling $10,450 to students from the Oklahoma City area.

Dexter G. Johnson Educational and Benevolent Trust, 204 North Robinson, Suite 900, Oklahoma City, OK

Loans to residents of Oklahoma.

Oregon

Bernard Daly Educational Fund, P.O. Box 351, Lakeview, OR 97630
Grants totaling $76,260 to twenty-eight residents of Lake County to study at Oregon schools.

Jenkins Student Loan Fund, U.S. Bank of Oregon, 321 SW 6th Avenue, P.O. Box 3168, Portland, OR 97208
Loans totaling $111,815 to Oregon students.

Ochoco Scholarship Fund, P.O. Box 668, Prineville, OR 97754
Grants totaling $28,800 to fifty-eight residents of Crook County, OR.

Ben Selling Scholarship Fund, First Interstate Bank of Oregon, P.O. Box 2971, Portland, OR 97208
Low-interest loans totaling $20,000 to Oregon residents attending Oregon schools.

Pennsylvania

Addison H. Gibson Foundation, Six PPG Place, Suite 860, Pittsburgh, PA 15222
Loans totaling $685,350 to 105 residents of western Pennsylvania who have completed at least one year of their academic program.

William Goldman Foundation, 1700 Walnut Street, Suite 800, Philadelphia, PA 19103
Grants totaling $64,250 to eight Philadelphia-area residents, to attend graduate or medical school in Philadelphia.

William J. McMannis and A. Haskell McMannis Educational Trust Fund, c/o PNC Bank, N.A., P.O. Box 8480, Erie, PA 16553
Ninety-seven grants totaling $114,275 to U.S. citizens, with preference given to residents of the environs of Erie, PA.

Anna M. Vincent Trust, c/o Mellon Bank, P.O. Box 7899, Philadelphia, PA 19101-7899
Grants totaling $225,875 to long-term residents of the Philadelphia area.

Jacques Weber Foundation, Scholarship Committee, P.O. Box 420, Bloomsburg, PA 17815
Grants totaling $66,577 to sixteen people residing within seventy miles of Bloomsburg, for the study of textiles.

Rhode Island

Paul O. and Mary Boghossian Foundation, c/o Rhode Island Hospital Trust National Bank, One Hospital Trust Plaza, Providence, RI 02903

Twenty-five grants totaling $37,500 to Rhode Island residents.

Mary E. Hodges Fund, 222 Tauton Avenue, East Providence, RI 02914-4556

Grants totaling $31,000 to individuals who have resided in Rhode Island for five or more years.

South Carolina

James F. Byrnes Foundation, P.O. Box 9596, Columbia, SC 29290

Grants totaling $105,250 to South Carolina residents who are orphans or have lost one parent.

Dr. Edgar Clay Doyle & Mary Cherry Doyle Memorial Fund, P.O. Box 1465, Taylors, SC 29687-1465

Grants to graduates of Oconee County, South Carolina high schools, attending South Carolina colleges.

Kitty M. Fairey Educational Fund, P.O. Box 1465, Taylors, SC 29687-1465

Grants totaling $155,232 to thirty-one South Carolina residents, attending four-year schools in South Carolina.

Foundation for The Carolinas, P.O. Box 34769, Charlotte, NC 28234-4769

Grants to students residing in South Carolina or North Carolina.

C. G. Fuller Foundation, c/o National Bank of South Carolina, N.A., P.O. Box 221509, Columbia, SC 29222-1509

Grants to South Carolina residents who are incoming freshmen at South Carolina schools.

Springs Foundation, P.O. Drawer 460, Lancaster, SC 29721

Interest-free loans totaling $326,019 to 174 undergraduates, medical students, and nursing students residing in Lancaster County or the townships of Fort Mill and Chester, SC.

South Dakota

The Hatterscheidt Foundation Inc., c/o First Bank–Aberdeen, P.O. Box 1000, Aberdeen, SD 57402-1000

Grants to graduates from certain high schools, and to students planning to attend Jamestown College or North Dakota State School of Science.

Howard Memorial Fund, 222 Midwest Capitol Building, Aberdeen, SD 57401

Thirty-three grants totaling $22,000 to students in Brown and Aberdeen Counties, SD.

Sioux Falls Area Foundation, 141 North Main Avenue, Suite 500, Sioux Falls, SD 57102

Twenty-four grants totaling $20,500 for South Dakota residents.

Tennessee

Wills Memorial Foundation, c/o Haywood County Executive, County Courthouse, Brownsville, TN 38012-2097

Grants totaling $35,000 to thirty-nine residents of Haywood County, Tennessee for study in health-related fields.

Texas

Ed E. and Gladys Hurley Foundation: see Louisiana.

Carl B. & Florence E. King Foundation, 5956 Sherry Lane, Suite 620, Dallas, TX 75225

Grants and loans totaling $111,500 to eighty-eight Texas high school students.

Franklin Lindsay Student Aid Fund, Texas Commerce Bank–Austin, Trust Div., P.O. Box 550, Austin, TX 78789-0001

Loans totaling $974,150 to 339 students attending Texas colleges and universities.

Minnie L. Maffett Scholarship Trust, c/o NationsBank of Texas, N.A., P.O. Box 831515, Dallas, TX 75283-1515

Grants totaling $35,050 to students from Limestone County, Texas schools, who will attend Texas colleges and universities.

Nettie Millhollon Educational Trust Estate, 309 West Saint Anna Street, P.O. Box 643, Stanton, TX 79782

Student loans totaling $176,600 to needy Texans.

Minnie Stevens Piper Foundation, GPM South Tower, Suite 200, 800 NW Loop 200, San Antonio, TX 78216-5699

Loans totaling $457,699 to Texas residents attending Texas schools.

The Abe & Annie Seibel Foundation, United States National Bank, Trust Dept., P.O. Box 179, Galveston, TX 77553

Almost $2 million in interest-free student loans to 1,476 graduates of Texas high schools, attending college in Texas.

Utah

Ruth Eleanor Bamberger & John Ernest Bamberger Memorial Foundation, 1201 Walker Building, Salt Lake City, UT 84111

Grants totaling $58,848 to fifty-six Utah residents in undergraduate programs.

Vermont

General Education Fund Inc., c/o The Farmers Trust Co., P.O. Box 1009, Burlington, VT 05402

Grants totaling $545,378 to Vermont residents, for undergraduate studies.

Olin Scott Fund Inc., 100 South Street, P.O. Box 1208, Bennington, VT 05201

Loans totaling $124,800 to young men from Bennington County, Vermont planning to attend Vermont colleges and universities.

Virginia

Ethel N. Bowen Foundation: see West Virginia.

Society of Cincinnati in Virginia Trust, P.O. Box 1357, Richmond, VA 23211

Grants totaling $51,000 to seventeen graduates of Virginia high schools.

Washington

Arthur & Doreen Parrett Scholarship Trust Fund, U.S. Bank of Washington, P.O. Box 720, Trust Division, Seattle, WA 98111-0720

Grants totaling $41,791 to nineteen Washington residents, for study in schools of engineering, science, medicine, and dentistry.

Poncin Scholarship Fund, c/o Seafirst Bank, Charitable Services, P.O. Box 24565, Seattle, WA 98124

Grants totaling $138,746 to individuals engaged in medical research at a Washington institution.

The Rachel Royston Permanent Scholarship Foundation of Alpha Sigma State of the Delta Kappa Gamma Society International, 2600 Century Square, 1501 Fourth Avenue, Seattle, WA 98101-1688

Ten grants totaling $12,000 to female educators residing in Washington, for graduate study.

West Virginia

Ethel N. Bowen Foundation, c/o First National Bank of Bluefield, 500 Federal Street, Bluefield, WV 24701

Grants totaling $247,667 to students from the coal mining areas of southern West Virginia and southwestern Virginia.

The Greater Kanawha Valley Foundation, 1426 Kanawha Boulevard East, Charleston, WV 25301

Grants totaling $393,221 to residents of West Virginia.

The Berkeley Minor & Susan Fontaine Minor Foundation, 1210 One Valley Square, Charleston, WV 25301

Nineteen grants totaling $105,506 to residents of West Virginia attending certain institutions.

Herschel C. Price Educational Foundation, P.O. Box 412, Huntington, WV 25708-0412

Grants totaling $133,000 to undergraduates residing in West Virginia or attending West Virginia colleges.

Wisconsin

Hobbs Foundation, P.O. Box 128, Eau Claire, WI 54702

Thirteen grants totaling $26,000 to residents of the Eau Claire, Wisconsin area.

Racine Educational Council, 310 Fifth Street, Room 101, Racine, WI 57403

Grants totaling $96,299 to residents of the Racine, Wisconsin area.

Wyoming

Dodd & Dorothy L. Bryan Foundation, P.O. Box 6287, Sheridan, WY 82801

Loans totaling $263,285 to 120 residents of certain Wyoming and Montana Counties.

Paul Stock Foundation, P.O. Box 2020, Cody, WY 82414

Grants totaling $131,564 to eighty-seven Wyoming residents, particularly from the Cody area.

Resources for Students with Disabilities

Students with disabilities may be interested in the following directory:

Financial Aid for the Disabled and Their Families, by Gail Ann Schlachter and R. David Weber, published by Reference Service Press of San Carlos, California.

This guide lists over 800 sources of funding for the disabled and their families, including scholarships, fellowships, loans, grants-in-aid, awards, and internships.

California-Hawaii Elks Major Project, Inc., Attn: Scholarship Committee, 5450 East Lamona Avenue, Fresno, CA 93727-2224

Twenty stipends of $2,000 per year (renewable for up to four years total) for postsecondary education, to disabled residents of California and Hawaii.

EIF Scholarship Fund, Electronic Industries Foundation, Attn: Scholarship Award Committee, 919 18th Street, NW, #900, Washington, DC 20006-5503

Six scholarships of $2,000 per year (renewable) to disabled students interested in preparing for careers in technical fields.

Lucille A. Abt Scholarship Awards, Alexander Graham Bell Association for the Deaf, 3417 Volta Place, NW, Washington, DC 20007-2778

Five scholarships of $1,000 each for postsecondary education, to profoundly deaf students.

Panasonic Young Soloists Award, Very Special Arts, Attn: Education Office, Kennedy Center, Washington, DC 20566

One or two awards of $10,000 to a permanently disabled vocalist or instrumentalist, for the purpose of broadening his or her musical experience or training.

Stanley E. Jackson Scholarship Awards, Foundation for Exceptional Children, 1920 Association Drive, Reston, VA 22091

Four scholarship awards of $1,000 each to students with disabilities.

Yumoto Ikueikai Scholarship, Asakusabashi 4-17-7, Taito-ku, Tokyo 111, Japan

Up to 10 scholarships to undergraduate disabled students wishing to study in Japan. The stipend is 15,000 yen (about $150 at presstime) per month, for the duration of the course of study.

CSU Forgivable Loan/Doctoral Incentive Program, California State University System, c/o Office of the Chancellor, 400 Golden Shore, Suite 218, Long Beach, CA 90802-4275

Loans of up to $10,000 per year (renewable for up to three years total) for up to 100 students at a time; restricted to disabled, minority, and female students interested in teaching at a CSU campus. The loan is forgiven 20% for each postdoctoral year of teaching at CSU; after five years of teaching at CSU, the entire loan is forgiven.

Gore Family Memorial Foundation Scholarships, c/o Sun Bank, P.O. Box 14728, Fort Lauderdale, FL 33302

Scholarships of up to $7,000 for undergraduate or graduate education, to severely disabled students.

NSF Graduate Fellowships, National Research Council, 2101 Constitution Avenue, Washington, DC 20418

Approximately 700 awards of $14,000 per year for three years, to disabled and other graduate students in the mathematical, physical, biological, engineering, and social sciences.

Chapter 7

Getting Money from Athletic Scholarships

Many millions of dollars in athletic scholarships go unclaimed each year, simply because no one applied for them, or because the schools in question couldn't find enough qualified applicants.

Before you reject this category because you are not a 350-pound left tackle or a seven-foot-three slam-dunker, consider the following brief history, which will explain why the situation now is very different from the way it was only a few years ago.

There are two historical factors that are relevant: the women's movement, and the athletic scandals that have been a fact of life at dozens of colleges since the 1970s.

The Effect of the Women's Movement

Until the late 1970s, it was all too common for colleges to have multi-million-dollar training facilities for the football team while the women's volleyball team practiced on a muddy lot with a clothesline stretched between two poles.

A law that took effect in 1978 decrees that schools must provide male and female athletes with equal "benefits and opportunities." This means separate (often) but equal (increasingly) practice facilities, equipment, number of coaches, number of games—and, significantly, scholarship money in correct proportion to the number of athletes. If there are sixty men on the football squad, and ten women on the bowling team, then one-sixth as much scholarship money should go to bowling women as to football men.

This isn't always the case, but the situation is much better than it was, and keeps improving.

The Effect of the Athletic Scandals

Everybody used to know anecdotes like the one about the star basketball player who was paid $1,000 a month to tear pages off the Dean's calendar. Most of them were true. There were incredible abuses of the academic process used to lure and keep outstanding athletes in the school.

In the aftermath of the exposés that filled sports pages in the late 1970s and early 1980s, the big winners were the so-called "minor" sports. There are now restrictions on how many scholarships can be awarded in the "major" sports (football, basketball, track and field, sometimes baseball), with requirements that the monies be distributed not *only* to women, but also to handball players, sailors, soccer players, archers, and so forth.

Another restriction limited payments to "just" tuition, room and board, books, and other academic expenses. No more big salaries for shoveling snow in July, and the Dean has to tear off his own calendar pages. This restriction will not seriously affect persons under 300 pounds and/or six-foot-eight.

An important side effect of this situation is that schools are not restricted in how they spend their *recruiting* time and effort, only their scholarship money. So they will often devote a major amount of both time and effort seeking out the best football players—but pay little or no attention to seeking out field hockey, squash, or badminton players. If some happen to turn up and ask for scholarship money, fine. If not, the money goes back into the general fund. No big deal. Wide World of Sports hasn't paid a nickel for the rights to collegiate field hockey.

The Four Main Reasons Why People Who Should Don't Apply for Athletic Scholarships

1. It doesn't occur to them that scholarships are available in their sport. See the long list below for inspiration in this regard.
2. They think they're not good enough. Simply not so, in many, many cases. Let's look at the numbers. There are, for example, 900 colleges and universities offering tennis scholarships for women. Conservatively, let's say 5,000 scholarships. To get one, then, you don't even have to be one of the top 5,000 female tennis players. You have to be one of the top 5,000 female tennis

players who want to go to college and who are academically qualified to do so.

Often, people downgrade their ability because they're not "even" tops in their own high school or club. Nonsense. There were twenty young women in the graduating class at the high school in our town, and *three* of them got four-year volleyball scholarships to major universities, including Stanford. You have to know enough to ask. There was a Philadelphia high school where all six seniors on the field hockey team received field hockey scholarships.

3. They think they're too old. But the scholarships depend on ability, not age. And in many of the so-called "minor" sports, there are many thirty-, forty-, even fifty-year-olds who can still shoot the gun, sail the boat, ride the horse, or lift the weights as well as anyone else on the team. A forty-three-year-old advertising man who decided to go back to finish his degree was delighted to learn that he qualified for a softball scholarship, based on abilities honed over years in the local pick-up league. The only qualification is that you are not a professional in your sport.

4. They don't know how to find out more. Minor sport scholarships are not widely advertised. Some information goes out over the grapevine (the "old coach" network), but much never reaches potential applicants.

It would take a book to list all the schools offering athletic scholarships, and the sports they offer them in. Fortunately, there is such a book. It is called *Athletic Scholarships: Thousand of Grants and over 200 Million Dollars for College-Bound Athletes*, by Andy Clark, published in 1993 by Facts on File, and available in many libraries. This useful book first lists all the schools, with their offerings, and then has a cross-index by sport, so you can instantly locate, for instance, all ninety-seven schools with women's lacrosse scholarships.

The Thirty-Eight Sports in Which Athletic Scholarships Are Available

This list may prove inspirational—and valuable, if you find your sport in it. We have indicated the number of colleges and universities offering scholarships to men and to women in each sport. For specific details, consult Clark's book, and/or write to the schools themselves or to the national associations in your sport (e.g., the U.S. Tennis Association).

Archery: 9 schools with scholarships for men, 1 for women.
Badminton: 10 for men, 15 for women.

Baseball: Over 1,000 for men, 42 for women.
Basketball: Over 1,000 for men, over 500 for women.
Bowling: 33 for men, 22 for women.
Crew: 53 for men, 22 for women.
Cross Country Running: Over 800 for men, over 400 for women.
Equestrian: 24 for men, 33 for women.
Fencing: 70 for men, 60 for women.
Field Hockey: 5 for men, over 250 for women.
Football: Over 600 for men, 6 for women.
Golf: Over 800 for men, over 200 for women.
Gymnastics: 85 for men, over 200 for women.
Handball: 2 for men, 3 for women.
Ice Hockey: 65 for men, 18 for women.
Lacrosse: 135 for men, 97 for women.
Martial Arts: 13 for men, 15 for women.
Polo: 1 for men, 1 for women.
Racquetball: 8 for men, 8 for women.
Riflery: 65 for men, 32 for women.
Rodeo: 24 for men, 17 for women.
Rugby: 32 for men, 12 for women.
Sailing: 31 for men, 19 for women.
Skiing, alpine: 40 for men, 40 for women.
Skiing, cross country: 36 for men, 37 for women.
Soccer: Over 600 for men, 52 for women.
Softball: 57 for men, over 600 for women.
Squash: 22 for men, 15 for women.
Swimming/Diving: Over 500 for men, over 500 for women.
Synchronized Swimming: 3 for men, 14 for women.
Tennis: Over 800 for men, over 900 for women.
Track and Field: Over 800 for men, over 300 for women.
Volleyball: 47 for men, over 900 for women.
Water Polo: 67 for men, 12 for women.
Water Skiing: 4 for men, 4 for women.
Weightlifting: 28 for men, 13 for women.
Wrestling: Over 400 for men, 1 for women.

Chapter
8

Getting Money from the Military

As an inducement to keep America strong, a strategy to have a better-educated military, and a reward for having served the country, substantial sums of educational funds are available each year to men and women who:

- have not yet entered the armed forces,
- are currently serving, or
- have been discharged from the service.

In addition, there are a great many scholarship opportunities available for *relatives* of people with military connections of various sorts.

Here is current information on funds available in these four categories. Bear in mind, however, that changes in policies and dollar amounts are frequent—tied, often, to the personnel situation in the military. When voluntary enlistments in the Navy, for instance, were way down, financial incentives to enlist, or to take Naval ROTC, were increased. When this strategy apparently worked, funds for the program were cut by two-thirds.

First, an Important Time vs. Money Consideration

The military doesn't give you something for nothing. They give you something for something, and what they get is hundreds, even thousands of hours of your life, through participation in part-time training activities and/or through a three-year enlistment commitment.

Is it worth it? Clearly for some people, even those who don't desperately want to help keep the world safe for democracy by serving in the Middle East, Central America, or other hot spots, the answer is yes. But for others, if they stopped to think it over carefully, they might well come to realize that they could have qualified for sufficient funds from other sources, without having to pledge the time to the armed forces. During the Gulf War, the news was full of human interest stories about people who had joined up to get an education, and never really believed, what with the end of the Cold War, that they would ever have to face combat. This is worth considering.

And when you factor into the equation the amount of money you would have earned in a civilian job, contrasted with the three years of military pay and benefits, you may well come to the decision that a nonmilitary approach is worth pursuing first. If that fails, the armed forces will likely still be there, ready to talk.

Before You Serve

The Military Academies

The three academies offer a full four-year scholarship to all students, including tuition, room and board, other living expenses, medical care, and clothing. In return, you give them nine years of your life: four while enrolled, and a five-year service obligation after graduation.

Each academy has between four and five thousand students, the majority of whom were nominated by members of the U.S. Congress, at the rate of two per congressional district per year.

Sons and daughters of armed forces personnel (active, retired, or deceased) may apply independently as "Presidentials"—100 per year are admitted to each academy. Children of a parent who died or was totally disabled in action may qualify separately. And all children of Medal of Honor winners are automatically eligible. For more information, write to:

Admissions Office
U.S. Military Academy
606 Thayer Road
West Point, NY 10996

Candidate Guidance Office
U.S. Naval Academy
Leahy Hall
Annapolis, MD 21402

Director of Cadet Admissions
U.S. Air Force Academy
Colorado Springs, CO 80840

Other Service Academies

Similar programs are available with the Coast Guard and the Merchant Marine. Graduates of the Coast Guard Academy also have a five-year obligation, while the Merchant Marine graduates have a variety of options available (but must serve in the Naval Reserve).

Director of Admissions
U.S. Coast Guard Academy
15 Mohegan Avenue
New London, CT 06320

Admissions Office
U.S. Merchant Marine Academy
Kings Point, NY 11024

ROTC Programs

Each service offers two programs for participants in the ROTC (Reserve Officers Training Corps). Both require that you take military courses as part of your college curriculum for four years, and serve a hitch on active duty after graduation. One program pays participants a $100 per month stipend for their junior and senior years only. The other offers two-, three-, or four-year scholarships (limited to 80 percent of tuition or $8,000, whichever is greater), plus the $100 a month. The latter are highly competitive; the former less so.

Less than 20 percent of colleges and universities offer ROTC programs these days. Lists and detailed information are available from the following offices:

U.S. Army ROTC Commander
Fort Monroe, VA 23651
800-USA-ROTC

U.S. Navy Opportunity Information Center
P.O. Box 5000
Clifton, NJ 07012
800-NAV-ROTC

U.S. Air Force ROTC Recruiting Division
Maxwell Air Force Base, AL 36112
800-423-USAF

U.S. Marine Corps Headquarters
Washington, DC 20380
800-NAV-ROTC

The National Guard and the Reserves

The Guard and the Reserves are only called to active duty in cases of emergency (military, civil, disasters, etc.). Otherwise, they attend monthly weekend training sessions and a summer camp for several weeks each year.

The U.S. government offers educational assistance of $1,000 a year to Guard members for up to four years. If you have a Guaranteed Student Loan (see Chapter 15), Guard membership can result in the loan being paid off at 15 percent of the total per year. From time to time, there are enlistment bonuses, and always there is pay for the weekend and summer training programs.

Finally, in most states (all but Arkansas, California, New York, Rhode Island, South Carolina, Tennessee, and Vermont) National Guard members get reduced tuition at the state universities.

While You Serve

If you enlist in the Army, Navy, Air Force, or Marines, you will have the opportunity to attend regular civilian colleges and universities, with the military paying as much as 90 percent of the tuition costs. The "GI Bill" also survives, although under a different name. And there are special, well-funded programs for doctors, nurses, and clinical psychologists.

Regular Civilian Colleges

The services have arrangements with hundreds of colleges and universities, whereby military people take regular classes on campus, or by correspondence, with anywhere from 25 percent to 90 percent of the costs paid by Uncle Sam. In the Army, the umbrella organization is the Servicemen's Opportunity College. In the Navy and Marines, it's the Campus for Achievement. And in the Air Force, it's the Community College of the Air Force.

The rules are not only long and somewhat complicated, they also change regularly. Full details are available from your friendly local recruiting office.

The Montgomery GI Bill

The Army allows you to accumulate money for your education through a generous matching funds program. You can sign up for an automatic payroll deduction of $100 per month. After twenty-four months of consecutive service, the Army contributes an additional $11,000. If you serve three years, this rises to a total of $16,000, and after four years to the maximum, $18,000. Contributions from the Veteran's Administration add $7,800 for a two-year enlistment or $9,600 for a four-year enlistment. So, in four years, you can accumulate $28,800 in money for college.

In addition, there are some large tuition bonuses available for people who choose (or are willing) to enroll in some of the less popular branches of the service (e.g., the infantry). Call 800-USA-ARMY for more information.

This all applies to people who enlisted after July 1, 1985. Those who enlisted before then are eligible for assistance too, through a program called VEAP (Veteran's Education Assistance Program). However, there is some talk that VEAP is going to be phased out, so those eligible should look into their benefits *now.*

Special Health-Related Programs

There are three programs that pay some or all of the expenses of people pursuing the study of medicine, nursing, or clinical psychology.

The armed forces have their own medical school with several hundred full-tuition scholarships per year to would-be doctors willing to enlist at the same time (which also provides lieutenants' pay—over $17,000 a year plus benefits—during schooling).

Admissions Office
Uniformed Services University of the Health Services
4301 Jones Bridge Road
Bethesda, MD 20814
(301) 295-3101

Three services offer scholarships covering all college costs plus some living expenses for students of medicine, osteopathy, and clinical psychology (Ph.D. level only), who enlist in their service.

Department of the Army (SGPE-PDM)
Student Programs Management
1900 Half Street SW
Washington, DC 20324
(703) 545-6700

Navy Department
Bureau of Medicine and Surgery (MED-214)
Washington, DC 20372
(703) 545-6700

U.S. Air Force
Health Professions Recruiting
Building 1413, Stop 44
Andrews Air Force Base, MD 20331
(703) 545-6700

Finally, would-be nurses who attend a nursing school that has an affiliation with an Army or Air Force ROTC unit may qualify for the ROTC Nurse Program, which pays full tuition plus a monthly stipend.

ROTC Nurse Program
Army ROTC
Fort Monroe, VA 23651

ROTC Nurse Program
Air Force ROTC Office of Public Affairs
Maxwell Air Force Base, AL 36112

Money For People with Military Relatives

Government Programs

The Survivors' and Dependents' Education Act provides up to $15,000 ($342 per month for forty-five months) for the educational expenses of children or spouses of veterans who either died, were totally disabled, or are missing in action as a result of their service.

The Compensation and Pension Program provides funds for the children of veterans with wartime service (World War I through Vietnam) who have died of non-service-connected causes.

Details of both these programs are generally available from financial aid counselors, or, failing that, from one's nearest American Legion Post.

The Army Emergency Relief Assistant Program provides up to $10,000 in loans (or $4,000 in scholarships) over four years for needy unmarried or dependent children of current or former Army members. Information from Army Emergency Relief, Department of the Army, 200 Stovall Street, Alexandria, VA 22332.

Private Programs

A good many scholarship programs exist through private (nongovernment) societies, to help pay college expenses for children (and occasionally spouses) of veterans. Many of these programs are described in materials available from the American Legion Education Program, Americanism and Children & Youth Division, Indianapolis, IN 46206.

Many of the programs are, in fact, offered by Legion chapters in all fifty states, Mexico, Puerto Rico, and the Canal Zone. The programs vary tremendously in scope (one award to dozens), amount ($50 to thousands of dollars), recipients (high school seniors to medical students), and what you have to do to get one. The American Legion pamphlet *Need a Lift?* gives all the particulars.

Here are a few of the other service-related programs:

The Air Force Aid Society offers low-interest loans up to $25,000 (over five years) to children or stepchildren of Air Force personnel. Information from the General Arnold Student Loan Program, Air Force Aid Society, 1735 North Lynn, Room 202, Arlington, VA 22209.

The Marine Corps Scholarship Foundation awards over 200 undergraduate scholarships a year to needy sons and daughters of current, former, or reservist Marines. Information from the Marine Corps Scholarship Foundation, 20 Nassau Street, Room 514, Princeton, NJ 08540.

The Navy Relief Society offers loans (no interest while in school, low interest thereafter) to unmarried dependent children of present or former Navy and Marine personnel. Funds are available for undergraduate, graduate, and vocational education. Details from the Navy Relief Society, 801 North Randolph Street, Suite 1228, Arlington, VA 22203.

The Retired Officers Association considers itself the source of last resort for sons, daughters, or wards of present or former officers of all uniformed services. After all other sources have been explored, the ROA will consider making interest-free loans to "fill the gap." This is for undergraduate education only. The Retired Officers Association is at 201 North Washington Street, Alexandria, VA 22314.

A great many other scholarships are available, quite a few for relatives of people who served in a particular theater of war (1st Marine Division, Gamewardens of Vietnam, with Chennault in China, the Confederate Army, the World War II Submarine Corps, etc.). All details to be found in *Need a Lift?*, published by the American Legion, Emblem Sales, P.O. Box 1050, Indianapolis, IN 46206. Cost: $3.

Getting Money from Big Corporations

Those five simple words up there describe what is not only the largest single source of money for college, but, by a huge margin, the most underused source of money.

Thousands of companies, big and small, offer to pay some or all of the school expenses of their employees (and, often, their employees' families).

How much money is available, and how much is actually claimed by employees? The numbers are astonishing, but true. The National Commission on Student Financial Assistance reports that:

About $7 billion in tuition assistance is available each year under benefit plans provided by employers for their workers, but *less than $400 million* is actually used.

The commission estimated that over 80 percent of all companies with more than 500 employees offer some form of tuition assistance—for example, support for training related to employees' jobs or aid for the education of family members.

Employer-sponsored programs are "overwhelmingly neglected" as a source of student aid, the report said, noting that *fewer than 5 percent of the employees eligible for such aid had used it in the last decade.*

If you're one of the 95 percent, passing up your share of that $6,600,000,000 going unclaimed this year, our only message is this:

YOU ARE ELIGIBLE. USE IT.

It is, in fact, not at all unreasonable to consider going to work for a company that *does* have a tuition-paying plan in effect. Why not let your employer pay the cost for you, and perhaps your family as well?

Most employer payments are channeled through various foundations, so the company will get tax benefits for its charitable work. A few companies even support members of the general public who either live nearby or have other connections with the company.

Here, just as a sampling, are some of the major corporate supporters of higher education. Remember that there are thousands more. A few prominent programs that have over the years been available to individuals other than employees are listed first.

Avon Products Foundation, 9 West 57th Street, New York, NY 10019

Awards $109,000 in scholarships to seventy-four individuals who are children of Avon employees.

Frank Gannett Newspaper Carrier Scholarships, Lincoln Tower, 15th Floor, Rochester, NY 14604.

Young men and women who have delivered any Gannett newspaper (they are a major nationwide chain) are eligible, as high school seniors, for more than 400 four-year $4,000 scholarships.

Food Fair Stores Foundation, 6500 North Andrews Avenue, Ft. Lauderdale, FL 33309.

Scholarships for employees, children, and residents of communities in which their stores are located.

Gemco Charitable and Scholarship Fund, 6565 Knott Avenue, Buena Park, CA 90620.

Scholarships in areas where Gemco stores are located, through a competition in which knowledge of economics and the free enterprise system is demonstrated.

Company Grants for Employees

Usually the foundation name is the same as, or similar to, the company name, with the word "Foundation" added, and the office is located at the main headquarters of the company.

On the list below, we have indicated any name variations, and have given the location of the foundation when it appears to be different from that of the sponsoring company.

There is, of course, no point in approaching any of the following unless you are, or in some cases were, an employee. Really. (After the first edition of this book came out—with the same advice—someone at GE wrote to tell us that they had received "a great number of letters" from students who had no connection whatsoever to the company. The only thing these letters accomplished—besides wasting the students' time and money—was annoying the GE employee who had to answer them.)

Abbott Laboratories: The Clara Abbott Foundation
Alcoa Foundation
American Can Company Foundation
American Electric Power System Educational Trust
American International: The Starr Foundation, 70 Pine Street, New York, NY 10270
American Optical Foundation
Andrew Corporation: Aileen S. Andrew Foundation
Bank of America–Giannini Foundation
Beneficial (Corporation) Foundation
Bibb (Company) Foundation
H & R Block Foundation, for children of employees and of franchise owners
Brown Group, Inc.: George W. Brown Foundation
Brunswick (Corporation) Foundation
Bulova Watch Company Foundation
Burlington Industries Foundation
Butler Manufacturing Company Foundation
Central Newspapers Foundation
Chaltham (Manufacturing Company) Foundation
Chubb (Corporation) Foundation
C.I.T. Financial Corporation: Ittleson Beneficial Fund, and Louis D. Beaumont Foundation, 650 Madison Avenue, New York, NY 10022
Citicorp: National City Foundation, 399 Park Avenue, New York, NY 10043
Colonial Life Insurance: same as **Chubb Foundation**
Communications Workers of America: Joseph Beirne Memorial Foundation, 1925 K Street, NW, Washington, DC 20006
Conoco Inc. Scholarship Committee
Conrad & Chandler Co.: Charles F. Bacon Trust, New England Merchants Bank, 28 State Street, Boston, MA 02107
Conrail: see **Penn Central**
Cummins Engine Foundation
Dan River Foundation
Downs (Carpet Company) Foundation
Dresser Industries: Dresser-Harbison Foundation Inc.
E-B Industries: Ensign-Bickford Foundation
Emery Air Freight Educational Foundation
Ernst & Whitney (Company) Foundation
Exxon: The Teagle Foundation, 30 Rockefeller Plaza, New York, NY 10112

Fieldcrest (Mills) Foundation
Ford Motor Company Fund (low-interest loans)
Gerber Baby Foods Funds
Goulds Pumps Foundation
Graniteville Co.: Gregg-Graniteville Foundation
Great Northern Nekoosa Foundation
Hallmark Educational Foundation (includes nephews, nieces, grandchildren)
Hall's (Motor Transit) Foundation
Heublein Foundation
J. L. Hudson Co.: Hudson-Webber Foundation
Inland Container Corporation Foundation
Inman Mills: Inman-Roverdale Foundation
Jacobus Company: Jacobus-Heritage Foundation
Walter Kidd and Co.: A.C.P. Foundation, 30 Bridlewood Road, Northbrook, IL 60062
Kimball International: The Habig Foundation, 1549 Royal Street, Jasper, IN 47546
Knudsen (Corporation) Foundation
Koch (Industries) Foundation
Marathon Oil Foundation
Marley (Company) Foundation
Martin Marietta Corporation Foundation
Maytag Company Foundation
McDonnell Douglas-West Personnel Community Service Inc.
Mead Johnson & Company
Merrill Lynch Scholarships
C. F. Mueller Co. Scholarship Foundation
National Machinery Foundation
National Presto Industries: Presto Foundation
Norton Simon Foundation
Outboard Marine Corp.: Ole Evinrude Foundation, 100 Sea Horse Drive, Waukegan, IL 60085
Penn Central: Women's Aid of the Penn Central, Conrail, Room 1010/6 Penn Center, Philadelphia, PA 19104
Pennwalt (Corporation) Foundation
Philip Morris Scholarship Award Program
Phillips Petroleum Educational Fund
Pinkerton Inc.: The ARW Foundation, 100 Church Street, New York, NY 10007
Pitney-Bowes Scholarships
Premier Industrial Foundation
Prentice-Hall: The Ettinger Foundation, 420 Lexington Avenue, Room 2320, New York, NY 10017

Quaker Oats Foundation
Sid Richardson Memorial Fund (former employees, their spouses or
    descendants)
Richman Brothers Foundation
Royal Crown Cola: Pickett & Hatcher Educational Fund, P.O. Box 8169,
    Columbus, GA 31908
Seagram College Scholarship Program
Southland Paper Mills Foundation
State Farms Companies Foundation
Superior Tube Co.: Superior-Pacific Fund
Tektronix Foundation
Textiles, Inc.: Myers-Ti-Caro Foundation, P.O. Box 699, Gastonia,
    NC 28052
Times-Mirror Company: Pfaffinger Foundation, Times Mirror Square,
    Los Angeles, CA 90053
Timken Company Educational Fund
**Towne Robinson Fastener Co.: Barney and Beatrice Keywell
    Foundation,** P.O. Box 232, Southfield, MI 48037
UOP Foundation
Walgreen Benefit Fund
Westinghouse Educational Foundation
Wisconsin Public Service Foundation
Wurlitzer Company: Fanny R. Wurlitzer Foundation

Chapter
10

Getting Money the Old-Fashioned Way: You Earn It

It is entirely possible, reasonable, and practical to consider making money while in college, with a small part-time business. Right away, an awful lot of people are scared off by the prospect. They think they know nothing about running a business; they don't know what kind of business to start anyway; and often they are intimidated by thoughts of failure, financial loss, or ridicule.

And yet, untold thousands of entrepreneurs in their teens and twenties (and even older) have managed to pay some, most, or all of their college costs through the profits of a spare-time enterprise they ran without interfering with their regular studies—and, in not a few cases, *enhancing* their regular studies, by doing, for instance, a business plan as a project in a business or economics class, then going out and implementing it in the real world.

Now we're not (necessarily) talking about large and ambitious ventures involving employees, lots of paperwork and bureaucracy, and the accompanying headaches. We're talking about making sandwiches or cookies in the late afternoon and delivering them to the dorms for evening snacks. We're talking about buying a high-speed tape cassette duplicating machine and making copies of cassettes (such as demo or audition tapes) for fellow students. We're talking about a telephone wake-up service, custom-made birthday cakes, library research, and pet sitting for traveling faculty.

Sure, some campus-launched businesses have grown into massive industries. The legend books are replete with tales of people like Mr. Hewlett and Mr. Packard who started while in college and ended up among the ten richest people in America. But far more important to the masses, and relevant to this book, are those ambitious and often hardworking folks who may sell 100 sandwiches a night at fifty cents profit each, and thereby reap $10,000 in the course of a school year.

How does one begin to think about doing this? You need ideas, you need inspiration, and you need good solid advice on procedures and methods. A good place to start is with books: this one, and two others I'll mention in a moment.

In the rest of this section, we'll list, with a very brief description where appropriate, thirty-eight of the most common ways people earn money *for* college while *in* college.

Some of these I have adapted from two excellent books on the subject. One, *The Student Entrepreneur's Guide,* was written by Brett Kingstone (McGraw Hill, 1989), who started a real business while a student (selling adjustable electric beds!) and lived to tell the tale in this helpful book. He really gets down to the nitty gritty, with lots of practical stuff on licenses and permits, fictitious business name registration, dealing with the government, banks, accountants, and so forth.

The other book is called *555 Ways to Earn Extra Money,* by Jay Conrad Levinson (Holt, Rinehart and Winston, 1982). Our old friend Jay has at least 427 very good ideas (all right, so we didn't like some of them) for part-time, spare-time, or even full-time businesses, many of which can be started by people with small amounts of money (even under $50) and/or limited business experience.

In addition to the 555 ways, there is a good deal of inspirational material on the secrets of earning money, and intelligent discussion of matters like commitment, determination, organization, and discipline.

Ways People Earn Money for College While in College

Babysitting: for pets, plants, even babies.
Balloon delivery.
Bartending for special events.
Birthday cakes: advertised with letters to parents, who then order them for campus delivery to their children.
Booking service: bands, speakers, campus entertainment.
Button-making: photo buttons with the inexpensive Badge-A-Minit™ machine.
Campus or town tours: for visiting parents, campus guests, tourists.
Companion or escort service: for students walking alone late at night, or for the elderly or handicapped.
Coupon books: selling space in them to local merchants and selling or giving discount coupon books to students. (Improbably, someone *else* named John Bear pioneered this idea at Stanford University.)
Delivering out-of-town papers: home delivery of the *London Times* or other special papers.

Desktop publishing: designing flyers (for businesses, bands, events), business cards, resumes, etc.

Dog walking.

Driving or chauffeuring: renting a Cadillac for $50 a day and then offering chauffeured service for $25 an hour.

Duplicating audio- or videotape cassettes: within the realm of what's legal, of course.

Food delivery: making your own sandwiches or cookies; delivery as an agent for pizza, deli supplies, etc.

Gardening: advice, or actually doing it.

House-sitting for traveling faculty or students.

Janitorial services.

Laundry: doing it for others in the campus laundry room; representing a dry cleaner on campus, with pick-up and delivery to rooms.

Local guidebook: preparing one for campus visitors: restaurants, sightseeing, etc.

Painting house numbers on curbs.

Painting, wallpapering: and other home handyperson services.

People matching services: dating, roommates, and rides.

Personal advice: clothing selection, color choices, makeup, etc., for the uncertain undergrad.

Photography: people, pets, homes, etc. One very successful plan involved taking photos (without being invited) of homes under construction, then selling albums of the photos to the owners.

Preparing picnic baskets: or entire picnic packages, with bike rental, blankets, frisbees, maps, etc.

Renting small appliances and other dorm needs: refrigerators, televisions, hot plates, carpets, etc. Maybe even small computers.

School spirit supplies: mugs, pennants, school emblem hats, T-shirts, jackets. A different and maybe classier line than that carried in the bookstore.

Sewing, mending, or darning.

Showing movies or videocassettes: classics, porno, etc.

Singing telegrams: by phone, in person, in costume, etc.

Specialty advertising goods: campus agent for a manufacturer of buttons, bumper stickers, key rings, imprinted ballpoint pens and pencils, other gimmickry.

Teaching things you do well: cooking, sewing, Rollerblading, calligraphy, etc.

Tutoring.

Typing and word-processing.

Valet parking service: faculty or students leave car with you; you park in distant lot and bicycle back.

Wake-up service: by telephone, usually. Also a reminder service for birthdays, anniversaries, other important dates.

Washing or waxing cars.

Chapter 11

Getting Money (or the Equivalent) Through Barter

The system of trade, or barter, is probably just about as old as humankind. ("I'll trade my club for your mammoth skin.") It often works well for both parties, with genuine benefits whose value may well exceed the number of dollars that otherwise would have had to be expended. This is especially true in the academic world, where enlightened schools have been trading tuition reductions (or eliminations) for all manner of services and skills they would not have been able to afford otherwise.

For example, a small college in the Midwest was eager to hire an experienced coach for their golf team—which would have cost them at least $25,000 a year. A local golf pro had a daughter interested in attending that school, which would have cost *him* at least $8,000 a year. A deal was struck whereby the pro spent three afternoons a week coaching to golf team, and his daughter's tuition and room expenses were waived; she paid only for food and books.

In recent years, more and more schools have been recognizing the value of barter, although it is still a very small factor in the big picture of academic economics. No school yet has a public or publicized program for encouraging barter, although dozens, perhaps hundreds have engaged in it, usually when approached by the potential student.

So there is nothing to be lost by trying. The most reassuring kind of situation, from the school's standpoint, is one in which there is some performance guarantee. If, for instance, the potential student proposes to recruit other students, on a commission basis, he or she might also agree to pay regular tuition *unless* a certain number of new students are located. A person who agrees to do certain work on the campus might negotiate for tuition to be reduced $10 for each hour of work—so the school knows it cannot lose money if the service is not rendered.

While many barter discussions begin between the potential student (or a family member) and the admissions department, some of the more successful ones involve the participation of a third party: an influential alumnus; an interested faculty member who knows how badly his department needs (for instance) a typewriter repairperson on call; the head of a fund-raising drive who can appreciate the potential in one's marketing skills, etc.

There is no right or wrong way to proceed. An agreement can be written or oral, formal or informal. It is important to be persistent. A number of people have told me that their initial casual inquiry was met by a response like, "Oh no, we couldn't do anything like that . . ."—but after a little persistence, often in getting through to a different person, negotiations were initiated.

Here are some of the barter arrangements that have been successful for both students and colleges:

Mechanical repair service. People who can fix office equipment, cars, and other machinery are very much in demand. Back when schools still relied on typewriters, John once saw over 100 of them collecting dust in the basement of a building, because the school simply couldn't afford to have them fixed or refurbished. These days, computer repair or MIS support services are similarly marketable, and trading such repair skill for school fees makes good sense for both parties.

Athletic coaching. Many schools would be delighted to field teams in certain "minor" sports, but cannot afford to hire a coach to establish and run the program. A person willing to devote ten to twenty hours a week doing this with volleyball, racquetball, field hockey, tennis, lacrosse, or dozens of other sports, in exchange for tuition for him or herself or a family member, would be welcomed in many places. Don't forget chess, backgammon, bridge, and go.

Academic coaching or teaching. Teaching a class, perhaps evenings or weekends, in your specialty, and/or spending some hours a week running remedial classes, or working one-on-one with students having problems.

Money-handling advice. The cash flow at even small schools is quite large, and many of them handle it extremely uncreatively, often badly. A financial advisor discovered that schools will keep literally millions of dollars in their checking accounts for long periods, not appreciating the value of using high-interest money-market accounts, even to store funds over a weekend. Similarly, many schools have multimillion-dollar endowment funds they are handling so conservatively, they are missing out on substantial profits. An experienced business executive or financial advisor could indeed trade valuable advice in return for tuition, etc.

Insurance advice. Insurance agents have been successful in advising schools on setting up or modifying student or faculty health or other plans, as well as introducing alumni insurance packages.

Travel agents. Passing on the commissions the agent receives from airlines, hotels, and such to the school.

Advertising and marketing advice. Schools are beginning to realize—too late in some cases—that they really *are* businesses, and cannot look down their noses at traditional business practices, including advertising and marketing to recruit students. Advertising, marketing, and direct mail practitioners are increasingly in demand.

Building trades. Plumbers, electricians, roofers, heating and air conditioning repairers, bricklayers, cement experts and the like, for obvious reasons.

Art and craft skills. Building furniture, painting murals, making stained glass windows, etc.

Gardening and landscaping.

Transportation. Flying or driving university people places in one's own vehicle. Transporting goods in a truck. One trucker based in a rural college town often returned with an empty truck from delivering goods to the big city. Returning with university supplies from city warehouses cost him almost nothing—and provided his son with reduced tuition.

Professional advice and assistance. Doctors, lawyers, nurses, dentists, architects, planners, and so forth are always in demand.

Entertainers. Performers and booking agents and friends of celebrities who can induce them to appear at school functions.

Writers. To teach writing classes. Or, in one creative solution, a well-known writer who was interested in earning a degree wrote a publishable dissertation, pledging the royalties to the school in lieu of tuition for his program.

Recruiters of students. This may be the most common and most valuable of all. Some schools encourage currently enrolled students or alumni to help promote the school to others in their community, business, etc. For each student who enrolls as a result of their efforts, they are paid a fee or commission, which can range from just a few dollars to many hundreds of dollars. Many students have been able to reduce their *own* tuitions to zero by this method.

Chapter
12

Getting Money from Work-Study Programs and Apprenticeships

Throughout history, people have been given jobs and/or an education in return for doing certain labors for the people who pay the bills. When the education is more of the craft or vocational sort, this is called an apprenticeship program; when it is of a more academic sort, it is called cooperative education.

Both arrangements offer ample opportunities to have someone else pay for a great deal of your educational expenses—and, in many cases, guarantee a job as well.

Cooperative Education

More than 200,000 students take part in cooperative education programs in any given year. The exact nature of the program varies from school to school, and even from company participant to company participant within a given school. A typical Bachelor's degree program will consist of one full year of classes to begin with. Then the next two (or three) years will have alternating semesters (or quarters) on campus and on the job. Normally it takes five years to complete the "four year" degree, during which time the typical student will earn more than $20,000 from his or her employer.

Other patterns include continuous half-time school and half-time employment, or in some instances, full-time school with the job only during vacation periods.

Some clever companies hire two cooperative students for one job, and they alternate roles: one in school, the other on the job each term. Sometimes both students will work during the summer.

Quite a few cooperative programs are available for graduate (Master's and Doctoral) students as well.

Roughly half of all cooperative education students stay on in a full-time job with their company after graduation, although there is rarely any requirement that they do so.

About 900 colleges and universities in the U.S. and Canada have cooperative education programs, and in a few of these, virtually every student is a participant. Those few are:

Cleveland State University
Drexel University (Philadelphia, PA)
GMI Engineering and Management Institute (Flint, MI)
Northeastern University (Boston, MA)
Shaw University (Raleigh, NC)
University of Cincinnati
University of Michigan (Dearborn campus)
Wilberforce University (Wilberforce, OH)

The largest single employer of work-study students is the federal government, with more than 15,000 participants in hundreds of different federal agencies, from the C.I.A. to the Smithsonian Institution to the Securities and Exchange Commission.

The two ways to learn about work-study programs are to write to the director of cooperative education at one of the 1000+ participating schools to learn what is available, or to ask the personnel department of companies or government agencies in which you have interest whether they participate in any such programs.

Information on work-study programs, including a list of all participating schools, is available from the National Commission for Cooperative Education, 360 Huntington Avenue, Boston, MA 02115. Phone: (617) 373-3770.

Apprenticeship Programs

Apprenticeship involves a written agreement between a worker and an employer or a trade association or union. The apprentice agrees to work for fairly low wages, and to attend relevant classes, in return for expert instruction from a master of the craft.

Apprenticeships are available in hundreds of different occupations, from carpentry to cooking, welding to nursing. The length of an apprenticeship agreement can run from one to seven years, with two or three being the most common.

Each occupation or trade has different rules and regulations regarding who may apply, but in general apprentices are between the ages of sixteen and twenty-five, with a high school diploma or equivalent.

Many apprenticeship programs are regulated by the government's Bureau of Apprenticeship and Training, whose main office is in the Department of Labor, Employment and Training Administration, Washington, DC 20213. In addition, there are regional offices in the federal office buildings in Atlanta, Boston, Chicago, Dallas, Denver, Kansas City, New York, Philadelphia, and Seattle.

In addition, twenty-three states have Apprenticeship Information Centers that maintain data on programs within that state, or sometimes within regions of the state (some states have two to six such centers). The federal office can direct you to the nearest state office.

Chapter 13

Getting Money from Miscellaneous Programs

The Job Corps

Of course, it isn't going to college, but for many people the Job Corps is a reasonable alternative, and for some it is the first step along a road that *does* lead to college.

The Job Corps was established as part of President Johnson's "Great Society" program in 1964 (remember that, fellow old-timers?) to train young people with difficult lives to take useful jobs in society.

Each year, thousands of people between the ages of sixteen and twenty-one spend from six to twenty-four months at a Job Corps Center learning new skills. Half are black, two-thirds are male, and virtually all are high school dropouts. Each participant receives room and board and a small monthly allowance.

Each state employment office has details, and so does the Job Corps Program, Employment and Training Administration, U.S. Department of Labor, Washington, DC 20210, (202) 219-8550.

National Merit Scholarship Program

The largest independent scholarship competition in the United States each year awards at least 1,500 one-time-only $1,000 scholarships and at least 1,500 four-year scholarships. Students from nearly 20,000 high schools compete by taking the Preliminary Scholastic Aptitude Test, which is also known as the National Merit Scholarship Qualifying Test, in the fall of the school year.

From the zillions who take the PSAT/NMSQT, the 50,000 highest scorers get a congratulatory letter, and any colleges to which they are applying will be notified. This may help with the admissions process.

The 15,000 highest scorers are declared to be semifinalists, which means another congratulatory letter, and a letter from their congressperson. The semifinalists' documents and applications are reviewed by human beings, not just the computer, and 5,000 finalists are chosen.

The entire program is financed by corporations, foundations, colleges, unions, and other large groups. It is administered entirely through high schools, and is for full-time students only. Informative literature can be secured from most high schools, or directly from the National Merit Scholarship Corporation, 1560 Sherman Avenue, Suite 200, Evanston, IL 60201-4897, (708) 866-5100.

A separate array of about 650 scholarships are available to African American students, who may participate in the regular National Merit competition *and* the special competition for African Americans at the same time. An informational bulletin is available from the National Achievement Scholarship Program for Outstanding Negro Students, One American Plaza, Evanston, IL 60201.

Chapter
14

Getting Money from Peculiar Sources and Off-the-Wall Schemes

Within certain broad restrictions, a person has the right to bequeath his or her money for any purpose whatsoever, no matter how peculiar or unusual. And that is why we have a whole raft of peculiar and unusual scholarships.

Many of them are not of broad interest. In fact, they are of such narrow interest that there may be only a small handful of people in the U.S. who would qualify for them—and have an interest in going to college.

There's no point in going into much detail here—but all details on these and others are available from the National Scholarship Research Service, as described on page 146.

Peculiar Scholarships

Convicted prostitutes in Seattle. A judge established this fund, which was, oddly, very little used.

People named Baxendale, Borden, Pennoyer, or Murphy. Scholarships available at Harvard.

People born on June 17, 1979. When they get old enough, 150 of them can claim a $1,500 scholarship from the Rochester Institute of Technology.

Former caddies from New Jersey. Scholarship from the New Jersey State Golf Association.

Children of glassblowers. Four $2,000 awards a year from the Glass Bottle Blowers Association of Media, Pennsylvania.

Wonder Woman Scholarships. Dozens of awards in the $2,000 to $5,000 range, to celebrate Wonder Woman's fortieth birthday, for talented women over forty.

Abstainers. $3,000 a year for students attending Bucknell University who don't use alcohol, drugs, cigarettes, or engage in strenuous sports.

Female helicopter pilots. $4,000 from the Whirly-Girls of Washington, DC.

Needy lefties. Four small scholarships for suchlike attending Juniata College.

Calf-roping scholars. $500 a year from the University of Arizona for people with high marks and calf-roping experience.

People named Defores or Leavenworth. $1,000 is waiting at Yale University.

Needy people interested in golf course turf. Twenty-five awards of $500 from the Golf Course Superintendents Association.

The Chutzpah Approach

Chutzpah is nerve. Cheek. Outrageous brashness. One Yiddish anthology defines it by the case of the man who killed his mother and father and then pleaded for mercy because he was an orphan.

In the world of scholarships, it could be defined by the young man who, on a cold winter day in East Lansing, Michigan in the late 1950s, dashed off a letter to Doris Duke that said, in effect, "It just isn't fair. There you are the richest woman in the world, who can buy anything you want, and here I am the poorest student in the world, who can't even afford the car I desperately need, much less next quarter's tuition."

The first thing that happened was a call from the local car dealer saying, "I've got a brand new Dodge for you, paid for by Doris Duke." The second thing was that his tuition was also paid.

Of the four or five super-rich people we've known, all but one said that even though they were quite well shielded from financial requests of all kinds, every so often some approach *did* break through to them, and whether because of the extreme cleverness of the approach, or often because of the extreme worthiness of the need, they actually did loosen their purse strings.

Nothing but time, energy, very modest cost, and perhaps damage to the ego, to be lost by trying. (Each year, *Forbes* magazine lists and describes the 400 richest people in America—and most of their addresses can be found in *Who's Who in America*.).

Chapter 15

Getting Money from Guaranteed Student Loans

The Stafford GSL Program

It used to be almost impossible for students to borrow money for college. Now it's easy—for those who qualify. While many millions of students *do* use this program (about 40 percent of all students, as a matter of fact), there are some five million more according to informed estimates who *could* but don't—either because they don't know about it, don't need it, couldn't understand it, or (in perhaps .00003 percent of the cases) felt guilty about taking advantage of their government.

Essentially what happens in the Stafford GSL (Guaranteed Student Loan) program is that the federal government guarantees to pay back the amount of loans made by others in case the student defaults, dies, or disappears.

The actual money, then, comes from local banks or other private lenders, from the state government, or occasionally from the school itself.

If you are already in school, or have chosen one (or several), their financial aid office will supply a list of available local lenders. At presstime, all of this information was as accurate as we could make it. However, over the past decade, the government has continually tinkered with the program, trying to bring interest rates, payment schedules, and eligibility into line with modern business procedures. In late 1995, the *Wall Street Journal* reported that the Republican-dominated Congress was pushing for deep funding cuts in student loans. Contact the financial aid office at any university for the latest.

The Amounts

Undergraduate students can borrow up to $6,625 a year for up to five years, up to a maximum of $46,000. Graduate students can borrow up to $18,500 a year up to a limit of $138,500. The limit includes any undergraduate loans.

The interest rate is well below the going rates, and is tied into ninety-one-day Treasury Bill rates. Generally they are under 10 percent per year. There is, however, a 5 percent loan origination fee, plus a 1 percent insurance charge. Thus if you borrow $5,000, you will actually get $4,455. Loans are divided into *subsidized,* in which Uncle Sam pays the interest on loans while the student is in school, and during any deferments and *unsubsidized,* in which interest accrues the entire time.

What It Takes to Qualify

Unsibsidized loans are available to anyone; there is no need to show financial need. For subsidized loan eligibility, there are elaborate formulas for calculating need—based on family income, other sources of scholarship money, number of children in college, and college fees. It is, for instance, the case that a student whose family income is over $65,000 may still get the maximum loan, if attending a more expensive school.

What About Repayment?

Yes, you *do* have to. These are loans, not gifts, and in recent years, the government has grown much more militant about pursuing and prosecuting those who don't repay.

You have to begin repaying the money within six months after leaving school, or dropping below half-time status as a student. You have from five to ten years to repay, with a minimum payment of $50 a month. At current (averages 9 percent) interest rates, for instance, a $10,000 loan will be repaid at $208 a month for five years, or $130 a month for ten years.

The only way to get out of repaying is to die, become totally disabled, or (as a significant number of recipients do) disappear. Declaring bankruptcy may not get you off the hook.

If you are unable to find a job after graduation, you can get a six-month extension, and if you enter certain internship or apprenticeship programs, you can delay (defer) repayment for up to two years.

Remember (see Chapter 8) that enlisting in the National Guard, the Reserves, or the active military can result in your loan being paid off by Uncle Sam in three to seven years.

Where to Begin

If you are in college, or have chosen one, probably the best place to start is with your school's financial aid department. They will have the appropriate forms, and can also supply a list of banks and other lenders in the vicinity.

You can also get the forms from the banks, or from the agency in your state or territory that handles GSLs.

The college's financial aid office will do the necessary calculations to determine and certify whether you qualify for a subsidized loan.

Federal Direct Student Loan

Quite unrelated to the Guaranteed Student Loan program, the federal government also makes billions of dollars a year available directly to schools, which the schools can then loan at very low interest rates to needy students. After graduation, a number of interesting options are available through which the loan need not be repaid at all.

The Amounts

The amounts and terms are the same as for Stafford and PLUS loans—the difference is that Uncle Sam is the lender rather than just the guarantor.

What It Takes to Qualify

Demonstrated need, as determined by the college to which you are applying.

Repayment

Repayment must begin within six months of earning the degree (or dropping below half-time status). You have ten years to pay off the loan, but if your income level is low you can get a ten-year extension. The minimum monthly payment is $30.

If, after earning the degree, you take a job teaching in any elementary, junior high, or high school serving primarily poor children (the government has a list), your entire loan will be canceled after five years, on a pro-rated basis (15 percent the first year, up to 30 percent the fifth). If you take a job teaching handicapped children in *any* school, your loan will be written off at the same rate, and if you teach in a Head Start program, it will be written off at 15 percent per year.

The same military repayments as for the Guaranteed Student Loans also apply, as described earlier in this chapter.

Where to Begin

It's out of your hands. Everything is done through the school's financial aid office. But not all schools participate in FDSL, and monies are not dispensed equally or even proportionally to schools. Apparently, less money goes to schools whose students have not repaid promptly in the past. But watch the newspapers. This one is a real political football. In general, the Republicans would like to eliminate the program entirely, and the Democrats have proposed increasing it.

PLUS Loans

PLUS loans are very similar to GSL loans, except here the parent borrows, and is responsible for the money, instead of the student. PLUS stands for Parent Loans to Undergraduate Students (there was a brief time when they were also available to graduate students, and the name was changed to Auxiliary Loan Program to Assist Students—ALAS—but now graduate students simply qualify for more unsubsidized Stafford loans.)

The Amounts

They is no fixed limit, as loans are based on cost of attendance minus other aid received. Need is never considered.

Repayment

Payments begin sixty days after the loan money is received. The term of the loan is from five to ten years, with a minimum monthly payment of $50.

Where to Begin

As with the Guaranteed Student Loans, either at the college financial aid office, at the banks or other local lenders, or at the appropriate state agency.

Federal Perkins Loans

These are need-based loans; the government supplies the money, the schools select the recipients and determine the amounts, based on their own calculations of need. How much a school has to offer is based on how much prior awardees have repaid, so some schools have large pools of Perkins money, others very little at all.

The Amounts

Undergraduates can borrow $3,000 a year, to a maximum of $15,000. Graduate students can borrow $5,000, to a maximum of $30,000 (including any money borrowed as an undergraduate). These amounts may be slightly higher if you attend a school that has a default rate of under 7.5% (which covers most traditional four-year schools). Basically, the government rewards schools with conscientious graduates by giving the successors more money.

What It Takes to Qualify

The program is based on demonstrated need, as determined by the school.

Repayment

Repayment begins nine months after graduation (or leaving school), and continues over up to ten years. The current interest rate is 5 percent. If you enlist in the Army, Army Reserve, or National Guard, the government will pay back a specified portion of your loan. Loan forgiveness is available in certain circumstances, such as for graduates who become full-time teachers in low-income areas, law enforcement or corrections officers, nurses or medical technicians, Peace Corps volunteers, and other positions that in some way benefit society.

Where to Begin

Ask the schools you're interested in about their Perkins default rate, how much money is available for new loans, and what their requirements are.

United Student Aid Loans

The USA Funds operate in much the same manner as the U.S. government, in the sense that they don't *make* loans, but they guarantee loans made by private lenders to both students and parents of students. USA is a private tax-exempt nonprofit corporation, receiving financial support from many large corporations. They also act as a mediator between many of these corporations and students, to arrange loans from the companies.

More than two million students have received billions of dollars in loans through this program. Many would not have qualified for other loans previously described. USA prides itself on helping people who could not find help elsewhere.

The Amounts

Undergraduate students can receive up to $3,000 a year for up to five years. Graduate students can be loaned up to $5,000 a year for up to five years.

What It Takes to Qualify

The program is based on demonstrated need, and inability to qualify under other loan programs.

Repayment

A minimum of $30 a month, with full repayment over a period of five to ten years. The interest rate is comparable to the PLUS loans.

Where to Begin

Either with the financial aid department of the school, with one of the 10,000 banks nationwide that participate in the program, or directly with United Student Aid Funds, 200 East 42nd Street, New York, NY 10017.

Sallie Mae: The Government's Loan Consolidation Service

This is one of those enlightened acts that gives one faith that there may be (some) hope for Big Government after all. A few years ago, the U.S. Congress, aware that students were having increasing difficulty paying off their student loans (especially when they had gotten money from more than one source), established the Student Loan Marketing Corporation, which quickly became known as Sallie Mae.

Sallie Mae offers the opportunity to do two things: to consolidate two or more student loans into a single loan, with a smaller monthly payment, and to extend the repayment period on loans (consolidated or not), which reduces the monthly payment amount.

The Amounts

Sallie Mae will now consolidate and/or extend qualifying loans in any amount.

What It Takes to Qualify

Holders of any federal loans—Stafford, Perkins, Direct, PLUS, or certain programs for medical students—are eligible. Married couples can consolidate their individual loans as well, provided they agree to be jointly liable even in the event they separate.

Repayment

Repayment extends over ten years for students who owe a total of under $7,500; it's twelve years for those owing between $7,500 and $10,000, fifteen years for $10,000 to $20,000, twenty for $20,000 to $40,000, twenty-five for $40,000 to $60,000, and thirty years for those fortunate few who owe over $60,000 in student loans. Monthly payments must be at least $50. The interest rate is the weighted average of the rates on all your loans, rounded up to the nearest percentage.

Where to Begin

At least four months before your first post-graduate payment is due, write to Student Loan Marketing Association, Smart Loan Organization Center, 12355 Sunrise Valley Drive, 5th Floor, Reston, VA 22091. The toll-free telephone number is (800) 524-9100.

Educational Credit Corporation

ECC is a private corporation, which offers a whole cafeteria of opportunities for students of all ages who wish to finance their education. This includes a Line of Credit Loan ($5,000 to $50,000) in which the borrower is given a book of checks to use for educational purposes; a Graduate Loan designed for college seniors or first-year graduate students; home equity loans; special academic credit cards; and so forth. ECC loans are not as good as government guaranteed loans because repayment begins at once instead of after the degree is earned, and because qualifying for them may be harder. On the other hand, they are better than government guaranteed loans because the money can be used for more diverse purposes (not just tuition and room and board); the upper limits can be higher and the time between application and disbursement of funds is generally much faster. You can reach ECC in California by calling (800) 477-4977.

Chapter
16

Getting Money from Federal and State Government Grants

Grants are different from loans in one rather significant way: *you don't have to pay them back!* Several billion dollars are given each year in the form of grants by the federal government, and billions more come from the individual states.

Pell Grant

Let's all hear it for Rhode Island Senator Claiborne Pell, who came up with the idea of outright government grants to worthy students. Over six billion dollars a year (the amount changes each year) goes to nearly four million students, thus an average of $1,500 per year each, with a range from $400 to $2,300. While the Pell program has borne the brunt of some budget cutting over the years, Congress has also been known to increase its appropriation so, at this juncture, it appears relatively safe. Beginning in 1995, there is a federally mandated cap at 3.9 million awards. As only 3.5 million eligible people applied in 1994, this should not be too much of a factor. Still, it doesn't hurt to apply early.

The procedure sounds wonderfully simple. You apply. You (or someone) calculates your Student Aid Index (SAI) number. If your number is low enough, you will receive Pell funds, in direct proportion to the lowness of this number.

In reality things are almost impossibly complex (not to mention highly frustrating). That SAI number is dependent on so many variables—your assets and income, your family's assets and income, home or farm equity, the rate of inflation, the number and financial status of people applying for grants this year, the funds available, the size of your family, your status in school, etc., etc., etc.—that one study found that more than *70 percent* of all Pell Grants were for the wrong amount!

The highly frustrating element is that the grants are usually not awarded until mid-to late spring—which is often too late to make other plans, if you do get turned down.

Since the decision is based entirely on the magic SAI number, it would be wonderful if you could calculate your own in advance, and thus know just where you stand.

Theoretically this is possible. Pell Grant information can be obtained from the Federal Student Aid Programs, P.O. Box 84, Washington, DC 20044, phone (800) 433-3243. (Pell Grants, incidentally, were originally known as BEOGs, for Basic Educational Opportunity Grants. The new name is the only simplification the program has undergone.)

Supplementary Educational Opportunity Grants

Each year, the federal government gives several hundred million dollars to participating schools. The schools, in turn, grant this money—$200 to $2,000 per person—to needy students to supplement other funds they may be getting.

The entire process is done through the college's financial aid department, or equivalent, and at their own discretion. The only relevant advice is to apply early, since this is a once-a-year largesse from Washington, and once it is gone, that's it for another year.

State Grants

Each of the fifty states offers a variety of scholarships and grants, as well as participating in and administering federal and other loan programs. Most of the programs are based on financial need, often combined with other criteria, such as grades in high school, test scores, and fields of intended study.

Over two billion dollars in state aid is available each year. In most cases, students are expected to apply for federal aid before or at the same time as state aid.

Each state has an office specifically to deal with all kinds of state grants and scholarships. Sometimes this is the same office that deals with loans, sometimes it is not. The following offices will be able to give you the information you need, or at least point you in the right direction:

Alabama

Alabama Commission on Higher Education
One Court Square, Suite 221
Montgomery, AL 36104-3584
(205) 269-2700

Alaska

Alaska Commission on Postsecondary Education
P.O. Box 110505
Juneau, AK 99811-0505
(907) 465-2854

Arizona

Arizona Commission for Postsecondary Education
2020 North Central Avenue, Suite 275
Phoenix, AZ 85004
(602) 229-2593

Arkansas

Arkansas Department of Higher Education
114 East Capitol Street
Little Rock, AR 72201-3818
(501) 324-9300

California

California Student Aid Commission
North Building, Suite 500
Sacramento, CA 94245
(916) 322-9267

Colorado

Colorado Commission on Postsecondary Education
1300 Broadway, 2nd Floor
Denver, CO 80203
(303) 866-2723

Connecticut

Connecticut Board of Higher Education
61 Woodland Street
Hartford, CT 06105-2391
(203) 566-2618

Delaware

Delaware Higher Education Commission
820 North French Street, 4th Floor
Wilmington, DE 19801
(302) 577-3240

District of Columbia

Department of Human Services
Office of Postsecondary Education, Research and Assistance
Suite 401
2100 Martin Luther King, Jr. Avenue, SE
Washington, DC 20020
(202) 727-3685

Florida

Florida Department of Education
Office of Student Financial Assistance
1344 Florida Education Center
Tallahassee, FL 32399-0400
(904) 488-1034

Georgia

Georgia Student Finance Authority
States Loans and Grants Division
2082 East Exchange Place, Suite 200
Tucker, GA 30084
(404) 493-5452

Hawaii

Hawaii State Postsecondary Education Commission
2444 Dole Street, Room 209
Honolulu, HI 96822
(808) 956-8213

Idaho

Office of the State Board of Education
650 West State Street, Room 307
Boise, ID 83720
(208) 334-2270

Illinois

Illinois Student Assistance Commission
1755 Lake Cook Road
Deerfield, IL 60015
(708) 948-8500

Indiana

State Student Assistance Commission of Indiana
150 West Market Street, Suite 500
Indianapolis, IN 46204
(317) 232-2350

Iowa

Iowa College Student Aid Commission
201 Jewitt Building
914 Grand Avenue
Des Moines, IA 50309
(515) 242-6703

Kansas

Kansas Board of Regents
400 South West 8th Street, Suite 609
Topeka, KS 66603
(913) 296-3517

Kentucky

Kentucky Higher Education Assistance Authority
1050 U.S. 127 South, Suite 102
Frankfort, KY 40601
(502) 564-4928

Louisiana

Louisiana Office of Student Financial Assistance
P.O. Box 91202
Baton Rouge, LA 70821-9202
(504) 922-1150

Maine

Finance Authority of Maine
83 Western Avenue
P.O. Box 949
Augusta, ME 04333-0949
(207) 289-2183

Maryland

Maryland State Scholarship Administration
16 Francis Street
Annapolis, MD 21401
(410) 974-2179

Massachusetts

Board of Regents of Higher Education
Scholarship Office
330 Stuart Street
Boston, MA 02116
(617) 727-9420

Michigan

Michigan Department of Education
Scholarship and Tuition Grant Program
P.O. Box 30008
Lansing, MI 48909
(517) 373-3394

Minnesota

Minnesota Higher Education Coordinating Board
Capital Square, Suite 400
550 Cedar Street
St. Paul, MN 55101
(612) 296-9657

Mississippi

Mississippi Postsecondary Education
Financial Assistance Board
3825 Ridgewood Road
Jackson, MS 39211-6453
(601) 982-6570

Missouri

Missouri Coordinating Board for Higher Education
101 Adams Street
Jefferson City, MO 65101
(314) 751-2361

Montana

Montana University System
2500 Broadway
Helena, MT 59620-3104
(406) 444-6594

Nebraska

Nebraska Coordinating Commission for Postsecondary Education
301 Centennial Mall South
P.O. Box 95005
Lincoln, NE 68509
(402) 471-2847

Nevada

State Department of Education
Capitol Complex
400 West King Street
Carson City, NV 89710
(702) 687-5915

New Hampshire

New Hampshire Postsecondary Education Commission
2 Industrial Park Drive
Concord, NH 03301
(603) 271-2555

New Jersey

New Jersey Department of Higher Education
Office of Student Assistance
4 Quakerbridge Plaza CN 540
Trenton, NJ 08625
(609) 588-3268

New Mexico

Commission on Higher Education
1068 Cerrillos Road
Santa Fe, NM 87501-4295
(505) 827-7383

New York

New York State Higher Education Services Corporation
One Commerce Plaza
Albany, NY 12255
(518) 473-0431

North Carolina

North Carolina State Education Assistance Authority
P.O. Box 2688
Chapel Hill, NC 27515
(919) 549-8614

North Dakota

North Dakota University System
North Dakota State Board of Higher Education
Student Financial Assistance Program
600 East Boulevard
Bismarck, ND 58505
(701) 224-4114

Ohio

Ohio Board of Regents
3600 State Office Tower
30 East Broad Street
Columbus, OH 43266-0417
(614) 466-1191

Oklahoma

Oklahoma State Regents for Higher Education
Oklahoma Tuition Aid Grant Program
P.O. Box 3020
Oklahoma City, OK 73101-3020
(405) 552-4356

Oregon

Oregon State Scholarship Commission
1500 Valley River Drive, Suite 100
Eugene, OR 97401
(503) 346-4166

Pennsylvania

Pennsylvania Higher Education Assistance Authority
660 Boas Street
Harrisburg, PA 17102
(717) 257-2800

Rhode Island

Rhode Island Higher Education Assistance Authority
560 Jefferson Boulevard
Warwick, RI 02886
(401) 277-2050

South Carolina

South Carolina Higher Education Tuition Grants Commission
P.O. Box 12159
Columbia, SC 29211
(803) 734-1200

South Dakota

South Dakota Department of Education and Cultural Affairs
700 Governors Drive
Pierre, SD 57501-2291
(605) 773-3134

Tennessee

Tennessee Student Assistance Corporation
404 James Robertson Parkway, Suite 1950
Nashville, TN 37243-0820
(615) 741-1346

Texas

Texas Higher Education Coordinating Board
7745 Chevy Chase Drive, Capital Station
Austin, TX 78752
(512) 483-6340

Utah

Utah State Board of Regents
Utah System of Higher Education
355 West North Temple
#3 Triad Center, Suite 550
Salt Lake City, UT 84180-1205
(801) 538-5247

Vermont

Vermont Student Assistance Corporation
Champlain Mill
P.O. Box 2000
Winooski, VT 05404
(802) 655-9602

Virginia

State Council for Higher Education for Virginia
101 North Fourteenth Street
Richmond, VA 23219
(804) 224-2623

Washington

Washington State Higher Education Coordinating Board
917 Lakeridge Way
Olympia, WA 98504
(206) 753-2210

West Virginia

Central Office of the State College and University Systems of West Virginia
1018 Kanawha Boulevard East, Suite 700
Charleston, WV 25301
(304) 247-1211

Wisconsin

Higher Education Aids Board
131 West Wilson Street, Suite 902
P.O. Box 7885
Madison, WI 53707
(608) 266-1660

Wyoming

Wyoming Community College Commission
Herschler Building 1W
122 West 25th Street
Cheyenne, WY 82002
(307) 777-7227

American Samoa

American Samoa Community College Board of Higher Education
c/o American Samoa Government
Pago Pago
American Samoa 96799-2609
(684) 699-9155

Guam

University of Guam Financial Aid Office
UOG Station
Mangilao, Guam 96923
(671) 734-4469

Northern Mariana Islands

Northern Marianas College
P.O. Box 1250
Saipan, MP 96950
(670) 234-6128

Puerto Rico

Council on Higher Education
Box 23305-UPR Station
Rio Piedras, PR 00931
(809) 758-3350

Trust Territory of the Pacific Islands

Office of Financial Aid
Micronesian Occupational College
P.O. Box 9
Koror, Republic of Palau, TT 96940

Virgin Islands

Virgin Islands Joint Boards of Education
P.O. Box 11900
St. Thomas, VI 00801
(809) 774-4546

Chapter 17

Getting Money from Fellowships, Grants-in-Aid, and Other Special Awards

There are a good many sources of money that do not fit neatly into other categories. Organizations of all kinds, both private and governmental, frequently make cash awards to students or potential students, based either on merit or on the results of a competition. Two good sources for this kind of information are *The Grants Register, 1995–97* edited by Lisa Williams, and published by the St. Martin's Press of New York; and *Financial Aid for Research and Creative Activities Abroad,* by Gail Ann Schlachter and R. David Weber, published by Reference Service Press of San Carlos, CA.

Here is a broad sampling of what you an expect to find. All awards are available to Americans. Many are available for Canadians, and some for anyone, worldwide. (There also exist, but are not listed here, many specific pairs-of-countries fellowships, such as ones for Malaysians to study in England, South Africans to study in Germany, and so on.)

AAUW Dissertation Fellowships, American Association of University Women Educational Foundation, 1111 16th Street, NW, Washington, DC 20036-4873

Fifty fellowships of $14,500 to female graduate students in the final year of writing the doctoral dissertation.

Abbey Major Scholarship, British School at Rome, Regent's College, Inner Circle, Regent's Park, London NW1 4NS, England

One scholarship of £3,330 plus board and lodging, to American and British graduate students of art and architecture, for a year of studio work in Rome.

Academy of Motion Picture Arts and Sciences, 8949 Wilshire Boulevard, Beverly Hills, CA 90211-1972

Up to five $25,000 fellowships to writers who have not sold a screen- or teleplay. These fellowships may not be used for pursuing a college or graduate degree.

Edward F. Albee Foundation, Inc., 14 Harrison Street, New York, NY 10013

Twenty-four awards to writers and painters, providing accommodation only at an artists' summer commune on Long Island.

All Saints Educational Trust, St. Katherine Cree Church, 86 Leadenhall Street, London EC3A 3DH, England

Eighty grants ranging from £500 to £2,000 to present and future teachers, for pursuing educational programs in the United Kingdom.

American Accounting Association, 5717 Bessie Drive, Sarasota, FL 34233-2399

Awards of $2,500 to undergraduates and Master's students, and $5,000 to PhD students, for the study of accounting.

American Institute of Baking, 1213 Bakers Way, Manhattan, KS 66502

Over twenty scholarships of up to $3,000 each awarded twice yearly, for the study of the scientific basis of baking and the technology of modern bakery production.

American Jewish Archives, 3101 Clifton Avenue, Cincinnati, OH 45220

A variety of fellowships of $1,000 to $2,000, to fund research and writing on American Jewish studies at the Archives in Cincinnati.

American Library Association, 50 East Huron Street, Chicago, IL 60611-2795

A variety of grants for research and study, and awards to recognize accomplishments relating to library science, reading, and intellectual freedom.

American Musicological Society, 201 South 34th Street, Philadelphia, PA 19104-6313

Six awards of $10,000 each for doctoral research in the various fields of music as a branch of learning and scholarship.

American Numismatic Society, Broadway at 155th Street, New York, NY 10032

A variety of fellowships ranging from $2,000 to $3,500, for the graduate study of numismatics and other humanistic fields in which numismatics plays a part.

American Oriental Society, Hatcher Graduate Library, University of Michigan, Ann Arbor, MI 48109-1205

One fellowship of $8,000 for graduate study of Chinese art.

American School of Classical Studies at Athens, 993 Lenox Drive, Suite 101, Lawrenceville, NJ 08648

A variety of fellowships, covering tuition, room and board, plus a stipend, for the study of classical philology and archaeology, post-classical Greek studies, and classical art history, in Athens.

American Society for Engineering Education, Suite 600, 1818 N Street, NW, Washington, DC 20036

Fifty fellowships of $16,000 each, plus tuition and other fees, for the graduate study of electrical and mechanical engineering, computer science, and a number of other subject areas of importance to the U.S. Navy.

American Society of Heating, Refrigerating and Air Conditioning Engineers, Inc., 1791 Tullie Circle, NE, Atlanta, GA 30329

Twelve to eighteen grants-in-aid of up to $7,500 each to graduate engineering students, for original scholarly research on the subjects of heating, refrigeration, air conditioning, and ventilation.

Austrian Government Summer Grants for Americans, Austrian Cultural Institute, 11 East 52nd Street, New York, NY 10022

Three grants of 10,000 Austrian schillings plus tuition reimbursement of up to AS7,000, to enable American students to spend a summer in Austria to study German or to conduct research.

Bijutsu Kogei Shinko Sato Kikin Fellowships, 5-9-39 Johmyoji, Kamakura-shi, Kanagawa 248, Japan 0467 23 0118

Up to three fellowships providing housing and a stipend of 80,000 yen per month, to students and scholars from outside Japan who wish to come to Japan to research arts and crafts.

Blues Heaven Foundation, Inc., 249 North Brand Boulevard, Glendale, CA 91203

One fellowship of $2,000 to be used at a Chicago-area college or university for the study of music, Afro-American studies, folklore, performing arts, or radio/TV/film.

Brookings Institution, 1775 Massachusetts Avenue, NW, Washington, DC 20036-2188

Fellowships of $15,000 each, to enable doctoral students to engage in a year of research at the Brookings Institution, in the areas of economics, government, and foreign policy.

Bundeskanzler Scholarships for Future American Leaders, Alexander von Humboldt Foundation, Attn: North American Office, 1350 Connecticut Avenue, NW, Suite 903, Washington, DC 20036

Ten scholarships of up to 5,500 Deutsche marks per month, plus travel expenses and some tuition, to students and young professionals interested in studying in Germany for a year.

Business and Professional Women's Foundation, 2012 Massachusetts Avenue, NW, Washington, DC 20036

Scholarships and loans ranging from $1,000 to $5,000, available to women, in a variety of business and professional fields.

CDS International, Inc., 330 7th Avenue, New York, NY 10001-5010

Fifty awards enabling Americans aged eighteen to twenty-four to spend a year studying and working in Germany.

Consortium for Graduate Study in Management, 12855 North Outer 40 Drive, Suite 100, St. Louis, MO 63141-8635

Approximately 170 fellowships covering tuition and fees, plus a $5,000 stipend, to African Americans, Hispanic Americans, and Native Americans pursuing an MBA degree.

Early American Industries Association, Inc., 1324 Shallcross Avenue, Wilmington, DE 19806

Three to five grants of $1,000 each for graduate and postgraduate work in the preservation and classification of obsolete tools and mechanical devices.

EBR Summer Travel Scholarships, American Schools of Oriental Research, 3301 North Charles Street, Baltimore, MD 21218

Sixteen grants of $1,000 each to help fund travel to and research in the Holy Land, by graduate and undergraduate students.

Eileen J. Garrett Scholarship Award, Parapsychology Foundation, Inc., 228 East 71st Street, New York, NY 10021

One scholarship of $3,000 to support research in parapsychology by a graduate or undergraduate student, either in the U.S. or abroad.

Electrical Women's Round Table, Inc., P.O. Box 292793, Nashville, TN 37229-2793

Two fellowships—one of $2,000 and one of $1,000—for women pursuing graduate degrees related to electrical energy.

Franklin and Eleanor Roosevelt Institution, Franklin D. Roosevelt Library, 511 Albany Post Road, Hyde Park, NY 12538

Fifteen to twenty grants-in-aid of up to $2,500, for research of the Roosevelt years and closely related subjects.

Fund for Theological Education, Inc., 475 Riverside Drive, Suite 832, New York, NY 10115-0008

A variety of scholarships to African Americans and Hispanic Americans for graduate studies in theology.

Fund for UFO Research, Inc., P.O. Box 277, Mt. Rainier, MD 70112

Grants to cover expenses of scientific research and public education projects relating to the phenomenon of unidentified flying objects.

Gladys Krieble Delmas Foundation, 521 Fifth Avenue, Suite 1612, New York, NY 10175-1699

Fifteen to twenty-five grants ranging from $500 to $2,500 for graduate study in Venice, Italy, in a number of subject areas.

Harper-Wood Studentship for English Poetry and Literature, St. John's College, Attn: Master's Secretary, Cambridge CB2 1TP, England

Studentship of up to £4,450 to a graduate of a university in the U.S. or the U.K., for graduate study of English poetry or literature in a foreign country.

Harry Frank Guggenheim Foundation, 527 Madison Avenue, New York, NY 10022-4301

Ten dissertation fellowships of $10,000 each, to Ph.D. candidates whose work includes the study of dominance, aggression, and violence.

Institute for Humane Studies, George Mason University, 4400 University Drive, Fairfax, VA 22030

A variety of fellowships, grants, and prizes for undergraduate, graduate, and postdoctoral studies in the areas of law, journalism, philosophy, and the social sciences.

Institute of Food Technologists, 221 North LaSalle Street, Chicago, IL 60601

Over one hundred scholarships for undergraduate and graduate study of food science and technology.

Institute of Irish Studies, Queen's University, 8 Fitzwilliam Street, Belfast BT9 6AW, Northern Ireland

Up to eight fellowships ranging from £5,874 to £15,798, for graduate research relating to Ireland, at the Institute in Belfast.

Institute of Jewish Studies, Hebrew University of Jerusalem, Mt. Scopus Campus, Jerusalem, Israel

Eight prizes ranging from $5,000 to $7,000, to fund graduate and postgraduate research at the Institute in Jerusalem..

Jacob's Pillow Dance Festival, Inc., Box 287, Lee, MA 01238

Scholarships covering tuition, and room and board, to enable dance students to participate in summer workshops at the Jacob's Pillow Dance Festival School.

Jewish Community Centers Association, 15 East 26th Street, New York, NY 10010

Eight to ten scholarships of up to $7,500 for graduate study toward the Master's degree, in preparation for employment at a Jewish Community Center.

Joseph Collins Foundation, 153 East 53rd Street, New York, NY 10022

Grants of up to $5,000 to medical students attending institutions east of the Mississippi River, who have broad cultural and artistic interests.

Manhattan School of Music, 120 Claremont Avenue, New York, NY 10027

Three hundred fifty scholarships for undergraduate and graduate study of music at the School.

Marshall Aid Commemoration Commission, Cultural Department, British Embassy, 3100 Massachusetts Avenue, NW, Washington, DC 20008

Up to forty scholarships of £13,500 per year, to enable intellectually distinguished young Americans to study for a degree at a British university.

Metropolitan Museum of Art, 1000 Fifth Avenue, New York, NY 10028-1098

A variety of paid internships are available to undergraduate and graduate students of art history and related fields.

National Association of Broadcasters, 1771 North Street, NW, Washington, DC 20036-2891

Grants of up to $5,000 to graduate students and senior undergraduates, for research of importance to the U.S. broadcast industry.

National Black Law Students Association, 1225 11th Street, NW, Washington, DC 20001

Six scholarships of $1,000 each to African American students entering law school.

National Endowment for the Humanities, Division of Research Programs, Room 318, 1100 Pennsylvania Avenue, NW, Washington, DC 20506

Hundreds of grants and fellowships to graduate students and scholars for study and research in the humanities.

National Federation of the Blind, Scholarship Committee, 814 Fourth Avenue, Suite 200, Grinnell, IA 50112

A number of scholarships ranging from $2,000 to $10,000 to legally blind undergraduates and graduate students.

National Medical Fellowships, Inc., 254 West 31st Street, 7th Floor, New York, NY 10001

Hundreds of fellowships ranging from $500 to $6,000 to minority medical students.

National Research Council, 2101 Constitution Avenue, Washington, DC 20418

Over one hundred fellowships for graduate and postdoctoral study and research, in the sciences and humanities.

National Right to Work Committee, 8001 Braddock Road, Suite 500, Springfield, VA 22160,

One scholarship of $2,000 to a student majoring in journalism or mass communication, who exemplifies the dedication to principle and high journalistic standards of William B. Ruggles. A 500-word essay on the right to work is required.

National Science Foundation/Graduate Research Fellowships, Oak Ridge Associated Universities, P.O. Box 3010, Oak Ridge, TN 37831-3010

One thousand fellowships for graduate study in the sciences.

Nurses' Educational Funds, Inc., 555 West 57th Street, New York, NY 10019

A number of fellowships and scholarships ranging from $2,500 to $10,000, to registered nurses, for graduate study.

Olivia James Traveling Fellowship, Archaeological Institute of America, 675 Commonwealth Avenue, Boston, MA 02215-1401

One fellowship of $15,000 to an American graduate student or scholar wishing to conduct research in Greece, the Aegean Islands, Sicily, southern Italy, Asia Minor, or Mesopotamia.

Phi Beta Kappa Society, 1811 Q Street, NW, Washington, DC 20009

One fellowship of $10,000 to an unmarried woman between the ages of twenty-five and thirty-five, for carrying out original research in French or Greek studies.

Philip Morris Scholarships for Artists of Color, Maryland Institute College of Art, 1300 West Mount Royal Avenue, Baltimore, MD 21217

Twenty scholarships of $10,000 per year each, tenable at five different institutions, to minority graduate students in a wide variety of creative fields.

Purina Mills, Inc., P.O. Box 66812, St. Louis, MO 63166-6812

Four fellowships of $12,500 each, for graduate study and research in the area of livestock and poultry production.

R. Howard Webster Fellowships, Delta Waterfowl and Wetlands Research Station, Rural Route 1, Portage La Prairie, Manitoba R1N 3A1, Canada

Five or more fellowships of 1,200 Canadian dollars per month, to support students conducting research in Canada on waterfowl and wetland ecology.

Samuel H. Kress Foundation, 174 East 80th Street, New York, NY 10021

A variety of fellowships ranging from $1,000 to $15,000, to doctoral students of art history, for travel and research.

San Francisco Conservatory of Music, 1201 Ortega Street, San Francisco, CA 94122

A number of scholarships ranging from $300 to $12,000, for the study of musical performance at the Conservatory.

Scripps Howard Foundation, P.O. Box 5380, Cincinnati, OH 45201-5380

A number of grants, fellowships, and scholarships of up to $3,000, to support undergraduate and graduate study of journalism and graphic arts.

Sigma Delta Epsilon/Graduate Women in Science, Inc., P.O. Box 19947, San Diego, CA 92159

Three to six fellowships of $2,000 to $3,000, to women doing research in chemistry or biology.

Sister Kenny Institute, 800 East 28th Street, Minneapolis, MN 55407

Nine monetary prizes for original artwork submitted to the International Art Show by Disabled Artists.

SME Education Foundation, P.O. Box 930, Dearborn, MI 48121

One scholarship of $5,000, for graduate study of manufacturing engineering.

Smithsonian Institution, 955 L'Enfant Plaza, Suite 7300, Washington, DC 20560

Graduate fellowships of up to $14,000, and postdoctoral fellowships of up to $35,000, for study and research at Smithsonian facilities, in a variety of fields.

Social Science Research Council, 605 Third Avenue, New York, NY 10158
A number of fellowships supporting international travel and research, in the humanities and social sciences.

Société des Professeurs Français et Francophone d'Amérique, 140 East 95th Street (1E), New York, NY 10128
Scholarships ranging from $1,200 to $12,000 to undergraduates, graduate students, and researchers, to fund study and research in France and Quebec.

Society for the Psychological Study of Social Issues, Central Office, P.O. Box 1248, Ann Arbor, MI 48106-1248
Grants-in-aid of up to $2,000 to graduate students, for scientific research of social problems.

Society of Exploration Geophysicists Foundation, Box 702740, Tulsa, OK 74170
Scholarships ranging from $500 to $3,000, to undergraduate and graduate students of geophysics and related earth sciences.

Soroptimist International of the Americas, 1616 Walnut Street, Philadelphia, PA 19103
Fifty-four awards of $3,000 each, to mature female heads of household pursuing an undergraduate education or vocational training.

Special Library Association, 1700 18th Street, Washington, DC 20009
Scholarships of up to $6,000, to graduate students in library and information science.

Sport Fishing Institute, 1010 Massachusetts Avenue, NW, Washington, DC 20001
Grants ranging from $500 to $5,000, to graduate students researching fish life history, fisheries management, or aquatic ecology pertinent to recreational fishing.

State Historical Society of Wisconsin, 816 State Street, Madison, WI 53706
Fellowships ranging from $2,000 to $5,000, for graduate research in American history, especially Wisconsin history.

Swedish Institute Guest Scholarships, P.O. Box 7434, S-103 91 Stockholm, Sweden
Scholarships of up to 6,700 Swedish krona, to assist non-Swedish students and researchers who want to come to Sweden to pursue specialized Swedish studies.

The American-Scandinavian Foundation, 725 Park Avenue, New York, NY 10021

An award of $2,000, plus publication in an issue of Scandinavian Review, *to the best English translation of poetry, fiction, drama, or literary prose written by a Scandinavian author since 1800.*

The Bunting Institute of Radcliffe College, 34 Concord Avenue, Cambridge, MA 02138

A variety of fellowships ranging from $3,000 to $30,000, available to women engaging in postdoctoral research, in a number of fields.

The Educational Foundation of the National Restaurant Association, 250 South Wacker Drive, Suite 1400, Chicago, IL 60606

Over one hundred awards ranging from $500 to $10,000, to students pursuing degrees in the food service/hospitality field.

The Harry S. Truman Library Institute, Independence, MO 64050

Fellowships of $16,000, and research grants of up to $2,500, to promote graduate scholarship relating to the Truman era.

The Herb Society of America, 9019 Kirtland Chardon Road, Mentor, OH 44060

Up to $5,000 for the scientific, academic, or artistic investigation of herbal plants.

The Kurt Weill Foundation for Music, 7 East 20 Street, 3rd Floor, New York, NY 10003

Grants and fellowships to support study and performance projects relating to the perpetuation of Kurt Weill's artistic legacy.

The Rotary Foundation, 1560 Sherman Avenue, Evanston, IL 60201

A variety of scholarships to undergraduates and graduate students, to cover expenses for international study and cultural exchange.

The Woodrow Wilson National Fellowship Foundation, CN 5281, Princeton, NJ 08543-5281

Forty fellowships of $12,500 each, for graduate research on religious or ethical values, in any field; fifteen grants of $1,200 for graduate research in women's studies.

Theodora Bosanquet Bursary Fund, 26 Moorfield, Canterbury, Kent CT2 7AN, England

One or two bursaries providing room and board in London, to a female undergraduate or graduate student from any country, who would like to come to London for a month to do research in English literature or history.

U.S. Army Center of Military History, Southeast Federal Center, Building 159, 5th Floor, Washington, DC 20374-5088

Two fellowships of $8,000 each, to promote graduate research and writing on the history of war on land.

U.S. Department of Education, Indian Fellowship Program, 400 Maryland Avenue, SW, Room 2177, Mail Stop 6335, Washington, DC 20202

Fellowships to Native American undergraduates and graduate students.

United Negro College Fund, Inc., 500 East 62nd Street, New York, NY 10021

Scholarships to students attending member colleges and universities, regardless of race, color, or creed.

United States Institute of Peace, 1550 M Street, NW, Suite 700, Washington, DC 20005-1708

Ten to twelve scholarships of $14,000 each, to doctoral students researching and writing on international conflict and peace.

University of York, International Office, Heslington, York YO1 5DD, England

Forty scholarships covering either one-third or one-sixth the cost of tuition, to enable overseas students to attend York, in either an undergraduate or graduate program.

Virginia Center for the Creative Arts, Sweet Briar, VA 24595

Three hundred fellowships covering residence at the Center for one to three months, to writers, painters, sculptors, composers, and photographers.

Washington University, Graduate School of Arts and Sciences, Campus Box 1187, 1 Brookings Drive, St. Louis, MO 63130

Fellowships to African Americans and women, for graduate study at Washington University.

Women's Research and Education Institute, 1700 18th Street, NW, #400, Washington, DC 20009

Eight fellowships of up to $11,500 to female graduate students interested in policy issues affecting women. The fellowship requires working thirty hours per week in a Congressional office as a legislative aide.

Women's Studio Workshop, P.O. Box 489, Rosendale, NY 12472

Grants and fellowships to female artists and writers, to cover residence at WSW, plus a stipend.

Woods Hole Oceanographic Institution, Education Office, Clark Laboratory, Woods Hole, MA 02543

Twenty to twenty-five fellowships of $3,800 plus travel allowance, to undergraduates and graduate students in the marine sciences, for a summer of research at Woods Hole.

Zonta International Foundation, Amelia Earhart Fellowship Awards, 557 West Randolph Street, Chicago, IL 60661-2206

Forty fellowships of $6,000 each to female graduate students of aerospace science and engineering.

Saving Money

Saving Money by Going to a Less Expensive or Foreign School

We realize that, at first glance, this suggestion looks about as useful as the advice we once found in a book of household hints: "To keep patio furniture from getting wet in the rain, bring it inside."

But it is surprising how many people get the idea in their heads that good schools have to be expensive—and thus, by inference, inexpensive schools cannot be as good.

College tuition is one of the very few areas of life where there is almost no connection between cost and value. The University of California at Berkeley costs less than one fifth as much as Stanford or Harvard, for instance, which is something like a Cadillac costing one fifth as much as a Lincoln. Comparable quality, vastly different price.

To learn that the College of Idaho costs five times as much as Oxford or Cambridge would be like learning that a Ford costs more than a Rolls-Royce.

All the above cars will get you where you're going. All of the schools will provide a good, usable degree. There simply is little correlation between the cost of the schools and the prestige of their credentials.

Rather than spending $50,000 or more in tuition over the course of a degree program, consider these three alternatives:

1. Choose a Less Expensive School

The logical alternative for many. Tuition costs at America's colleges and universities range from nearly zero to more than $20,000 a year. Tuition information may be found in all the standard college guides (*Cass and Birnbaum, Barron's, Peterson's, Patterson's, Lovejoy's*, etc.), and, of course, in each school's catalog or bulletin. Since tuition costs rarely change (i.e., go up) more than 10 percent per year, you can make a pretty good estimate of what you're in for over the course of your stay at any given school.

2. Start Inexpensively, Then Transfer

If it is really important, for whatever reason, to have a degree from one of the expensive schools, consider the alternative, pursued by many, of attending an inexpensive junior college, community college, or state school for the first two (or even three) years, then transferring in to the expensive school to complete your degree work.

About half the colleges and universities in America permit Bachelor's degree students to attend only for the last year in order to earn their degree. Another 45 percent have a two-year minimum enrollment, and only a handful require three or four years on their campuses.

3. Consider a Foreign University

Since virtually all foreign universities are government owned and operated, they do not have the financial problems of many American schools. Also, in many parts of the world, higher education is heavily subsidized, so that the student pays little (or, in some cases, none) of the cost of his or her tuition or expenses.

Further, there are quite a few scholarships, fellowships, and other funding opportunities available for people from one country who wish to study in another. Often, these will cover not only school costs, but room and board, and some or all of the travel costs.

The best source of information on study abroad is called *Study Abroad*, a splendid book published every two years by UNESCO, and available at most libraries, some bookstores, or by mail from the UN bookstore. For details, call the bookstore at (212) 963-7680.

Study Abroad describes all the United Nations and various intergovernmental agency scholarships available. (A few samples are given at the end of this section.) Then there are about 500 pages of detailed descriptions of scholarships offered by each country of the world, either for its own citizens to study somewhere else, or for people from somewhere else to come and study there. This is followed by another 500 pages on specific courses of study offered by the universities and institutes of each country, specifically designed for, or available to, people from other countries.

An important source of scholarship and other funding for Americans is the various "friendship" organizations that exist to promote understanding between, for example, the people of the U.S. and of Austria. Some offer awards covering one year overseas, others for entire degree programs over three or four years.

Some Intergovernmental Associations That Award Scholarships

There are many international intergovernmental associations that award scholarships, but the following three are the only ones of which the U.S. is a member, making U.S. citizens eligible.

Colombo Plan Bureau, P.O. Box 596, Colombo 4, Sri Lanka. Awards in all fields that contribute to socio-economic development for citizens of Colombo Plan countries, which include the U.S., Malaysia, Indonesia, Burma, Pakistan, Korea, and many others in Asia.

Commission of the European Communities, 200 Rue de la Loi, 1049 Bruxelles, Belgium. Funds for scholars anywhere who are studying integration in Europe.

Organization of American States, Washington D.C. 20006, for citizens of OAS nations (U.S. included) in all fields but medicine.

Some International Organizations That Award Scholarships

(The few that follow give a small indication of the kind of organizations listed in *Study Abroad*.)

International Federation of University Women, 37 Quai Wilson, 1201 Geneve, Switzerland. Scholarships for members worldwide to study humanities, social science, or natural science in another country.

Hague Academy of International Law, Peace Palace, Den Haag, Netherlands. Thirty-seven scholarships a year for students between ages twenty and thirty to study law and political science in The Hague, with studies in either English or French.

Universal Esperanto Association, Nieuwe Binnenweg 176, 3015BJ Rotterdam, Netherlands. Scholarships covering studies, lodging, some travel, for people between eighteen and twenty-nine and fluent in Esperanto, to study the world Esperanto movement.

The International Friendship Societies

Many of these organizations offer scholarships for student exchanges between the U.S. and their country; others can facilitate the legal or bureaucratic problems that sometimes arise in such matters. Some are official government agencies, some are private foundations, and some are in a grey area in between.

Afghanistan: Afghan-American Educational Commission, P.O. Box 3124, Kabul, Afghanistan.

Argentina: Commission for Educational Exchange between the U.S.A. and Argentine Republic, c/o The American Embassy, Buenos Aires, Argentina.

Australia: Australian-American Educational Foundation, P.O. Box 1559, Canberra City, A.C.T., Australia.

Austria: Austrian Institute, 11 East 52nd Street, New York NY 10022; also Austrian-American Educational Commission, Vienna, 8 Shemidgasse 14, Austria.

Belgium: Belgian-American Educational Foundation, 420 Lexington Avenue, New York, NY 10017; also Commission for Educational Exchange between the U.S.A., Belgium, and Luxembourg, 29 Boulevard du Regent, Regentlaan, Brussels 1000, Belgium.

Brazil: Commission for Educational Exchange between the U.S.A. and Brazil, c/o The American Embassy, Brasilia, Brazil.

Chile: Commission for Educational Exchange between the U.S.A. and Chile, Casilla 2121, Santiago, Chile.

Colombia: Commission for Educational Exchange between the U.S.A. and Colombia, Icetex Building Penthouse, Carrera 3A, Apartado Aero 5735, Bogota, Colombia.

Cyprus: Commission for Educational Exchange between the U.S.A. and Cyprus, D. Severis Avenue, Kanaris Street, Nicosia, Cyprus.

Denmark: American-Scandinavian Foundation, 127 East 73rd Street, New York, NY 10021; also U.S. Educational Foundation in Denmark, Raadhosstraede 3, Copenhagen 1466, Denmark.

Ecuador: Commission for Educational Exchange between the U.S.A. and Ecuador, c/o The American Embassy, Quito, Ecuador.

Finland: American-Scandinavian Foundation, 127 East 73rd Street, New York, NY 10022; also U.S. Educational Foundation in Finland, c/o The American Embassy, Helsinki, Finland.

France: Alliance Française de New York, 22 East 60th Street, New York, NY 10022; also Franco-American Commission for Education Exchange, 9 Rue Chardin, Paris, France.

Germany: Commission for Educational Exchange between the U.S.A. and the Federal Republic of Germany, 53 Bonn-Bad Godesberg, Theaterplatz 1a, West Germany; also The Bavarian State Government Exchange Program, c/o Institute of International Education, 809 U.N. Plaza, New York, NY 10017.

Ghana: Commission for Educational Exchange between the U.S.A. and Ghana, c/o The American Embassy, Accra, Ghana.

Greece: U.S. Educational Foundation in Greece, 15 Valaoritou Street, 3rd Floor, Athens 134, Greece.

Iceland: U.S. Educational Foundation in Iceland, Nesvegur 16, P.O. Box 7133, Reykjavik, Iceland.

Ireland: Scholarship Exchange Board in Ireland, 80 St. Stephen's Green, Dublin 2, Ireland.

Israel: U.S.-Israel Educational Foundation, 71 Hayarkon Street, P.O. Box 26160, Tel Aviv, Israel.

Italy: Commission for Educational Exchange between Italy and the U.S.A., Via Copagni 16, V Rome 00187, Italy.

Japan: U.S. Educational Commission in Japan, 2nd Floor, Sanno Grand Building, 14:2, 2-Chome, Nagatha-cho, Chiyoda-Ky, Tokyo 100, Japan.

Korea: Korean-American Educational Commission, c/o The American Embassy, Seoul, Korea.

Liberia: U.S. Educational and Cultural Foundation in Liberia, c/o The American Embassy, Monrovia, Liberia.

Luxembourg: see Belgium.

Malaysia: Commission for Educational Exchange between the U.S.A. and Malaysia, Room 406, Lee Wah Bank Building, Old Market Square, Kuala Lumpur, Malaysia.

Nepal: Foundation for Educational Exchange between the U.S.A. and Nepal, Kingsway, Kathmandu, Nepal.

Netherlands: Netherlands-American Commission for Educational Exchange, Prinsegracth 919, Amsterdam, Netherlands.

New Zealand: New Zealand-U.S. Educational Foundation, Box 3465, Chief Post Office, Wellington C.1., New Zealand.

Norway: American-Scandinavian Foundation, 127 East 73rd Street, New York, NY 10021; also Norway-American Association, Drammen-svn 20 V, Oslo 2, Norway; also U.S. Educational Foundation in Norway, Kedre, Vollgate 3, Oslo, Norway.

Pakistan: U.S. Educational Foundation in Pakistan, 511 Ramna 6/4, 84th Street, Ataturk Avenue, Islamabad, Pakistan.

Paraguay: Commission for Educational Exchange between the U.S.A. and Paraguay, c/o The American Embassy, Asuncio, Paraguay.

Peru: Commission for Educational Exchange between the U.S.A. and Peru, Maximo Abril 599, Lima, Peru.

Philippines: Philippina-America Educational Foundation, Teodorica Apartmens, 1148 Roxas Boulevard, Manila, Room 301, Philippines.

Poland: Kosciuszko Foundation, 15 East 65th Street, New York, NY 10021.

Portugal: Luso-American Educational Commission, Av. Elias Garcia, 59-5, Lisbon 1, Portugal.

Russia: International Research and Exchanges Board, 110 East 59th Street, New York, NY 10022.

Sweden: American-Scandinavian Foundation, 127 East 73rd Street, New York, NY 10021; Texas-Swedish Cultural Foundation, P.O. Box 27459, Houston, TX 77027; Sweden-American Foundation, Greu Turegatan 14, 1146 Stockholm, Sweden; and U.S. Educational Commission in Sweden, Norrmalmstorg 1, 11146 Stockholm, Sweden.

Taiwan: U.S. Educational Foundation in the Republic of China, 54 Chinan Road, Section III, Taipei, Taiwan.

Thailand: U.S. Educational Foundation, Cultural Affairs Officer, The American Embassy, Bangkok, Thailand.

Turkey: Commission for Educational Exchange between the U.S.A. and Turkey, 3/8 Celikkale Sokak, Kizily, Ankara, Turkey.

United Kingdom: English Speaking Union of the U.S., 16 East 69th Street, New York, NY 10021; U.S.-U.K. Educational Commission, 26 Dover Street, London W1X 4DX, England.

Uruguay: Commission for Educational Exchange between the U.S.A. and Uruguay, Paraguay 1217, Montevideo, Uruguay.

Venezuela: North American Association of Venezuela, Edif Blandin, Piso 2, Calle Guaicaipuro Final Avenue, Casanova El Rosal, Apartado 60835, Caracas, Venezuela.

Finally, an excellent source of information on foreign study, and all its ramifications, is the Institute of International Education, IIE Books, 809 U.N. Plaza, New York, NY 10017. Call (212) 984-5412 for a brochure. They offer many useful publications, with titles such as *Academic Year Abroad, Vacation Study Abroad, Money for International Exchange in the Arts,* etc., as well as a free pamphlet, *Basic Facts on Study Abroad,* which outlines the essentials for U.S. students.

Chapter
19

Saving Money by Dealing with Nontraditional Schools

There are three reasons for going to college: to get a degree, to get an education, and to have the experience of being at college. The three are often quite unrelated. It is entirely possible to end up with any one without the other two, or any two without the third.

If the degree is the important thing, as it is for most people going to college, then it is possible to save a great deal of money by dealing with a nontraditional school or a nontraditional program within a traditional college or university.

The nontraditional approach encompasses a wide variety of things. It is much easier to say what it is *not*. It is not sitting in class and lectures day after day, year after year, to amass enough credit to earn a degree.

Here are the ways degrees can be earned nontraditionally:

Credit (and degrees) for life experience learning. A small percentage of schools agree with the logical notion that it doesn't really matter *where* you learned something. If you know it, you should get credit for it. If you took four years of German in college and achieved fluency, you would earn something like thirty-six semester hours of credit. So if you became just as fluent in German by learning it from your grandmother, or from a Berlitz course, why shouldn't you get the same thirty-six units? Most schools won't do this, but some will, for all demonstrable nonschool learning.

Credit (and degrees) by examination. If you can pass the final examination in a course, why bother to take the course? More than half the colleges and universities in America subscribe to this belief and give anywhere from 25 percent to 100 percent of the credit needed for a degree for passing any of several hundred standard examinations. It is possible, for instance, to complete an entire year of college in one day, for a cost of less than $150!

Credit (and degrees) by correspondence study. Seventy American and Canadian universities offer a total of thousands of courses by home study. The cost is low, you can remain employed, and the work you do at *any* school can be applied to the credits needed for a degree at those relatively few schools that award degrees entirely through home study.

Credit (and degrees) for independent study projects. There are some schools that acknowledge the fact that many things people do in the "real world" demonstrate their scholarly and creative abilities even better than work done in school. Such enlightened institutions give substantial credit for writing symphonies or business plans, dramatic performances, developing and implementing a curriculum plan, counseling, research while traveling, preaching, teaching, and a great deal more. Often the Master's thesis or Doctoral dissertation takes the form of an independent study project that is, entirely or in part, something you might well have done *anyway* as a part of ordinary life.

Accelerated programs. Most traditional students attend college classes about fifteen hours a week, thirty to thirty-five weeks a year, and take four years to earn a Bachelor's or a medical degree, two to three years for a Master's or Doctorate. But there are programs in which students attend classes that are twice as long, don't have long summer and Christmas vacations, and complete the "four year" program in twenty-four to thirty months. This may or may not cost less in school fees, but it gets you out into (or back in) the job market a great deal sooner.

Part-time programs. Hundreds of universities offer degrees, including Doctorates and law degrees, entirely through either evening or weekend courses, thus allowing students to keep their full-time jobs. A few dozen schools offer a "weekend college" program in which students move onto campus Friday evening and live the life of a student until Sunday evening, when they return to their other world.

All of the above approaches are described in some detail in a truly wonderful book called *Bears' Guide to Earning College Degrees Nontraditionally* brought to you by the very same authors who wrote the book you're holding now. This 324-page large-sized volume evaluates hundreds of nontraditional Bachelor's, Master's, Doctorate, Law, and Medical degree programs worldwide, and also describes, in a separate section, the several hundred illegal and dangerous degree mills that take advantage of people's desires for degrees by selling them anything they want for a cost of $3 to $3,000. A free 16-page descriptive booklet is available from John Bear, P.O. Box 7070FM, Berkeley, California 94707.

Here are some of the best examples of schools and programs in the six categories described above:

Credit (and Degrees) for Life Experience Learning

Hundreds of schools give *some* credit, but only a handful give a great deal, and only three major accredited colleges will award their Bachelor's degrees *entirely* for work done elsewhere.

They are:

- University of the State of New York, Regents College, 7 Columbia Circle, Albany, NY 12203.
- Thomas Edison State College, 101 West State Street, Trenton, NJ 08608.
- Charter Oak College, 66 Cedar Street, Newington, CT 06111-2646.

Credit (and Degrees) by Examination

The above-named three schools also award their degrees entirely by examination, while others allow as much as 80 percent to 90 percent of the necessary credit to be earned this way. Very few schools have their own examinations. Rather, they require you to take standard exams held regularly at hundreds of locations nationwide by two independent private testing agencies.

One series is called CLEP—the College-Level Examination Program, administered by the College Entrance Examination Board, P.O. Box 1824, Princeton, NJ 08540. The other is called PEP—the Proficiency Examination Program, administered by American College Testing Program, P.O. Box 168, Iowa City, IA 52240.

Although schools differ somewhat in their policies, in general you earn four to six semester units for each hour of CLEP or PEP test you take. Since 120 units are normally required for the degree, you can achieve this in a total of twenty to twenty-four hours of tests.

The fastest and least expensive way to earn credit and the degree entirely by examination—but probably the most difficult—is via the Graduate Record Exam, administered by Educational Testing Service, P.O. Box 955, Princeton, NJ 08541. The GRE is given in twenty subjects, and each exam is worth thirty-nine semester units at some schools, hence a grand total of three exams for the Bachelor's degree!

Some other schools that give substantial credit for examinations include:

- Western Illinois University, Nontraditional Programs, 309 Sherman Hall, Macomb, IL 61455.
- University of Iowa, Division of Continuing Education, W400 Seashore Hall, Iowa City, IA 52242.
- Indiana University, External Degree Program, 1300 West Michigan Street, Student Union G-025M, Indianapolis, IN 46205.

Credit and Degrees by Correspondence Study

Only a few of the seventy universities offering correspondence courses also award degrees by correspondence, while others (including the first three named on page 133) award *their* degrees for correspondence work done *elsewhere.*

Two accredited schools offer innovative correspondence programs leading to the Bachelor's *and* Master's degree:

- California State University, 1000 East Victoria Street, Dominguez Hills, CA 90747. The External Degree Program in Humanities offers the M.A. by correspondence in history, literature, philosophy, music, and art.
- Empire State College (of the State University of New York system), Center for Distance Learning, Saratoga Springs, NY 12866. Offers home study and degrees through learning modules in more than 100 subject areas.

The seventy schools offering correspondence courses are listed in *College Degrees by Mail*, and described in some detail in a book called *The Independent Study Catalog*, published by Peterson's Guide, P.O. Box 2123, Princeton, NJ 08540.

The three American universities with the largest and most diverse offerings by correspondence study (although none offer degrees by correspondence) are:

- Brigham Young University, Independent Study, 210 HRCB, Provo, UT 84602.
- University of California, Independent Study Department, 2223 Fulton Street, Berkeley, CA 94720.
- University of Wisconsin, Independent Study, 209 Extension Building, 432 North Lake Street, Madison, WI 53706. (Wisconsin is one of the few schools offering not only academic but vocational and technical courses by correspondence as well.)

The largest correspondence university in the world is the University of South Africa, P.O. Box 392, Muckleneuk Ridge, Pretoria 0001, South Africa. Bachelor's, Master's, and Doctorates may be earned without ever having to travel to South Africa, and North American students may enroll.

Credit and Degrees for Independent Study Projects

In addition to most of the schools already mentioned, the following are among those worthy of attention:

- California State University, Dominguez Hills, 1000 East Victoria Street, Carson, CA 90747. The External Degree Program in Humanities offers an accredited, totally-nonresident M.A. in history, art, music, philosophy, religion, and related areas, at modest cost.
- Union Institute, 440 East McMillan Street, Cincinnati, OH 45206-1947 has a widely accepted and fully accredited Ph.D. program based on attendance at weekly meetings held at various locations around the country, plus completion of a "Product Demonstrating Excellence" in your field.
- Heriot-Watt University, Edinburgh, Scotland offers an international M.B.A. entirely through distance learning, also at modest cost. John Bear has opened a U.S. agency office for this program at 6921 Stockton Avenue, El Cerrito, CA 94530.

There are dozens of other good alternatives for degrees by nonresident or very short residential study. All are described and evaluated in *Bears' Guide*.

Accelerated, Part-Time, and Weekend Programs

There are hundreds of them, all requiring regular attendance on the campus. The most efficient approach (other, perhaps, than looking at *College Degrees by Mail*) is to telephone local colleges and universities, and inquire. If they don't have what you seek, they should be aware of what their local competition is offering, and may even tell you.

Chapter
20

Saving Money with the Advanced Placement Program

Since most colleges charge somewhere between $50 and $500 per semester unit, the opportunity to earn credit at the rate of $5 to $7 per unit is indeed a good way to "find money for college."

The Advanced Placement Program, administered by The College Board, consists of more than twenty examinations, each of which is accepted by more than 1,000 colleges as the equivalent of a freshman-level course in that subject.

The examinations are designed to be the equivalent of the final examinations given at the end of a typical one-year advanced (i.e., college-level) high school course in that subject. So the fee of $72 per exam "buys" the equivalent of one-quarter to one-fifth of an entire freshman year. Four or five exam passes and many schools will enroll you as a sophomore, rather than a freshman.

Many high schools offer special advanced placement courses to prepare students for the exams, but you don't have to take them; people not in high school, or in schools without courses, may sign up directly with The College Board, 45 Columbus Aveue, New York, NY 10023-6992; phone (212) 713-8000.

Advanced Placement exams are available in art (studio or history), biology, calculus (two exams), chemistry, computer science, economics, English (two exams), French (language or literature), German language, history (U.S. or European), Latin (two exams), music, physics (three exams), psychology, Spanish (language or literature), and statistics.

Saving Money by Not Going to College

It seems almost trivial to mention, yet it is surprising how many people are so set on the idea of going to college, it never even occurs to them to consider *not* going to college.

There are two unrelated kinds of reasons to give serious thought to the notion of not going (or at least not going *now*), especially if money is a problem. One relates to the usefulness of degrees, the other to the long-term economics of not going, compared with the financial rewards of going.

Not Going Because the Degree May Not Be So Useful

Most people pursue a degree for one of five reasons:

1. To get a job (or a better job).
2. To get an increase in salary in the present job.
3. For admission to graduate school or other studies requiring a degree.
4. For self-satisfaction or to gain respect from others.
5. To fool people with a degree from one of the many illegal degree mills.

There is not much we can say to people in the last two categories. For category four, I suggest that the least expensive school that meets your standards is probably appropriate, since almost no one will ever ask where the degree is from anyway. For category five, there is a genuine risk of being arrested, jailed, and fined. Using a fake degree in public is like putting a time bomb in your resumé; you never know when it might "go off." If you must have a degree or title, a $20 Doctorate from the Universal Life Church (601 Third Street, Modesto, CA 95351)—legal because degrees from churches are at best minimally regulated—is far safer than a $2,500 Doctorate from a clever degree mill.

For categories one and two, there have been serious questions raised lately regarding the usefulness of degrees in the job marketplace. In the 1960s, for instance, we were told by "experts" that the nation was facing a great teacher shortage, and hundreds of thousands of people thereupon pursued degrees in education.

However, as Alexander Mood wrote in a report for the Carnegie Commission, "It has been evident for some time to professors of education that they were training far more teachers than would ever find jobs teaching school, but few of them bothered to mention that fact to their students. That is understandable, of course, since their incomes depend on having students."

The same situation exists in the business world. A survey by the *Wall Street Journal* found many highly disillusioned M.B.A.'s. "Graduate school was a waste of time," said one typical M.B.A. holder after ten months of fruitless job hunting. "I wouldn't have come here and spent all that money if I had known it would be this tight," said another jobless M.B.A.

These problems are by no means just in the fields of education and business. There are seven communications graduates for every job opening in that field; twelve anthropology graduates per available job; and so it goes.

As Alexander Mood put it, ". . . in the past, the investment in higher education did at least pay off for most students, that is, they did get access to higher-status jobs; now for the first time in history, a college degree is being judged by many parents and students as not worth the price. They see too many of last year's graduates unable to find work, or taking jobs ordinarily regarded as suitable for high school graduates . . . Moreover, this is not a temporary phenomenon."

This point of view, especially when taken with the financial arguments following, should at least add "don't go" to the list of alternatives seriously to be considered.

Not Going in Order to Make More Money

Author Caroline Bird presents a most intriguing and ingenious argument for *not* going to college in her book *The Case Against College* (see

Bibliography section). We are adapting her 1976 calculations to the realities of the present day.

First, let's consider the actual cost of going to college for four years. Starting with the 1992–1993 school year, the average cost (tuition, room and board, books) is about $70,000 for private schools, a mere $40,000 for public schools. (At a conservative 6 percent per year inflation rates these figures will rise, respectively, to $118,000 and $81,000 by the year 2000!)

Second, let's consider the actual monetary value of a degree. Here, from recent census data, are average lifetime earnings from age eighteen to retirement:

high school graduates: $576,000
Bachelor's degree: $852,000
Master's degree: $1,140,000
Doctorate: $1,380,000

It would appear, at first glance, that for the eighteen-year-old poised on the brink of either college or job, the Bachelor's degree will be worth close to $300,000.

But let's say the eighteen-year-old entered the job market instead, and invested $12,500 a year that otherwise would have gone for college expenses in a money market account each year for four years. At a 10 percent interest rate, that money would total almost exactly three and a half million dollars by retirement age, sixty-five.

In other words (or numbers), by investing the college money conservatively between the ages of eighteen and twenty-two, and never doing a day's work, our hypothetical student ends up with more than ten times the salary increment expected by earning the Bachelor's degree, and nearly triple the lifetime earnings of a typical Ph.D.

Of course many people don't have the money to invest between eighteen and twenty-two—although a big chunk of it could come by living very prudently while working for those four years, especially if supplemented by funds from parents, in lieu of college expenses.

More and more people may be agreeing with a report by Dr. J. H. Holloman of M.I.T. and Richard Freeman of Harvard, concluding that "large numbers of young people, for the first time, are likely to obtain less schooling . . . than their parents."

Chapter
22

Saving Money with Financial, Real Estate and Tax Schemes and Gambits

Businesspeople, tax consultants, financial planners, and others who earn their living by telling the rest of us what to do with our money have come up with a number of different approaches to help pay for college. Some of these may be just right for certain people in certain situations; others may be ineffective or even disastrous.

How can you tell the difference? The best advice is to get a second opinion and then a third. Don't rely just on the purveyor or supporter of the scheme, and most emphatically don't rely on this book. These matters are far more complex and sophisticated than can be covered here—even if there *were* definitive and undeniably correct opinions, which there aren't.

Savings Plans

Some banks and savings and loans offer "special" savings plans to put away college money. These have as much to do with education as "Christmas clubs" have to do with Christmas. Despite the names, the "Edu-Plans" and "Edu-Chex" and "Edu-Scam" deals are usually nothing more than low-interest savings accounts that encourage, remind, or require you to put a little (or big) something aside each month.

The Clifford Trust and the Crown Loan

These two tax-saving schemes are designed to divert funds from high-tax-bracket parents to low-tax-bracket children.

The Clifford Trust allows a parent to establish a trust, to run for at least ten years. Any money that is earned during this period goes to the lower-tax-bracket child. After the ten-year or longer period, the assets in the trust revert to the parent.

The money initially used to start the trust is a gift to the trust, for the benefit of the child, and thus comes under gift tax rules. By a sophisticated calculation, it turns out that about $16,000 can be given as a tax-free gift per child, each year.

The Crown Loan situation permits, under certain circumstances, making an interest free loan to one's children. When set up properly, there are said to be pleasant tax benefits for both parents and child. However, the IRS watches these matters very closely.

Once again, it is vigorously recommended that competent legal and tax advisory aid be sought before proceeding with either of these options.

Consider, also, the ramifications of either of these schemes on other financial aid pursuits. When colleges or other potential lenders (or givers) calculate the financial position of an entire family, the assets of the child are given much more weight—often seven times as much—as the assets of the parent. It may well turn out that making the child wealthier (on paper, at least) as the beneficiary of a Clifford Trust or Crown Loan, may result in said child not being eligible for scholarships or loans from others.

The Real Estate Gambit

Essentially the philosophy goes like this:

1. If a child goes to college for four years, that's forty-eight months of renting a place to live, which is likely to cost a never-to-be-seen-again $10,000 to $20,000.

2. That sum of money is used as the down payment on a house near the campus.

3. Rooms in said house are rented to other students, with the rental money going to make at least part, and often all, of the mortgage payment. If there's an excess, it can also go toward paying tuition.

4. At the end of four years, the house is sold. Assuming a modest 5 percent per year rate of appreciation, the increase in value is likely to pay most or all of the four years' worth of tuition expenses.

This is a situation in which we must be grateful that so many colleges and universities, large and small, were established in small, rural, or out-of-the-way towns where real estate bargains are still to be found. The economics are less workable in the Berkeleys and Cambridges of the world, but in Iowa City and East Lansing and Champaign and Pullman and hundreds of other smaller-town sites of very large schools, it is not only possible, but being done regularly.

In fact, the gambit is even more rewarding for those who follow the advice of those get-rich-quick-in-real-estate gurus who advocate buying structurally sound but cosmetically run-down or ugly "fixer-uppers" (often with small down payments) and fixing them up. Offering tenants (or your own offspring) reduced rents in return for their upfixing time and skill may pay off nicely at sale time.

Parents without enough cash, or students without supporting parents, can still bring this off by going in with others. Three or four partners in a house that can hold seven or eight residents are still able to make the down payment, and to collect enough rent from others to meet the monthly payments and taxes and upkeep.

Reference

Chapter
23

Scholarship Search Services

This is a potentially good idea—some clever entrepreneurs have researched the world of available scholarships, entered thousands of them in their computers, and, for a fee, will endeavor to match your needs and qualifications with the available awards.

The main advantage of this approach is that someone else has done most of the work for you. There is no way an individual can possibly learn about, and keep tabs on all of the more-than-20,000 different organizations, agencies, and schools giving scholarships. For their relatively modest fee they guarantee to find a small number of relevant scholarships (the range in fees is from about $40 to $200), or they will refund your fee. In practice, however, there are enough scholarships for which almost *anyone* is eligible, so that it is rarely necessary to make refunds.

In July 1992, the *Chronicle of Higher Education* published an article entitled "States hope to curb scholarship-search companies that prey on anxious students and their families." Author Michele Collison says that "Attorney Generals are scrambling to keep up with complaints that have been pouring into their offices about scholarship companies. They say the agencies promise to find anxious students and parents thousands of dollars in 'unclaimed' scholarship money [but] usually, respondents end up with little more than a list of financial-aid programs and scholarships."

The *Chronicle* points out that the information for which these services charge up to $200 is often available free through colleges and high school districts that subscribe to CASHE: the College Aid Sources for Higher Education. CASHE has a database of 150,000 sources of grants, loans, scholarships, fellowships, and work-study programs. Schools typically pay several thousand dollars a year to subscribe, then offer the service free to students or potential students. It seems reasonable to ask your local high school district, or the financial aid office of a college in which you have interest, if they are subscribers to CASHE.

If you wish to see what a scholarship search can offer, you may wish to look at the National Scholarship Research Service, a pioneer in this field. You can reach them at (707) 546-6777 or 2280 Airport Boulevard, Santa Rosa, CA 95403.

Prentice-Hall and Career Press have published the **National Scholarship Research Service** databank in two volumes, one for undergraduate sources and one for graduate programs. Thus it is possible to do your own research in the NSRS databank, at a cost considerably less than having the search done for you (especially if you can find these books in the library). Check the Bibliography for details.

In addition to the scholarship search services, Peterson's Guides offers a software package that may be of assistance to some scholarship-seekers. For information, contact the **College Selection Service**, Peterson's Guides, P.O. Box 2123, Princeton, NJ 08540-2123, (609) 243-9111. This guide to select schools is available in IBM format only, for $170 (for the 1996 edition). It offers assistance to individuals seeking scholarship programs, relevant athletic scholarships, and other financial aid, in addition to broader college selection issues.

In summary, the main value of these services is that they save you time and energy that you would have to spend doing research on your own. For the equivalent of one or two days' college costs, you will, at the very least, get some valuable leads based on extensive and ongoing research, and at best you will end up with substantial sums of money to help finance your college education.

Chapter
24

Bibliography

Note: There are dozens of books about scholarships on the market, and there is a certain sameness to many of them. They cover the well-known government and private sources, but offer little in the way of creative or unusual approaches, and they are not listed here. The following publications may have useful aspects for some people in some situations. If the publication is easily obtainable in (or special-ordered by) a bookstore, we have given just the author and publisher. If it must be ordered from an organization, the address and phone number for so doing are listed.

AFL-CIO Guide to Union-Sponsored Scholarships. (Washington DC: AFL-CIO Department of Education). A comprehensive list of scholarship and aid programs available for union members and their families. Free to union members (non-members pay $3.00) from the AFL-CIO Department of Education, 815 16th Street NW, Washington, DC 20006; (202) 637-5000.

Graduate Admissions Essays: What Works, What Doesn't, and Why, Donald Asher. (Berkeley, CA: Ten Speed Press, 1991).

The Case Against College, Caroline Bird. (New York, NY: D. McKay Co.).

College Cost Book, The College Board. (New York, NY: The College Board). Published annually, it does for $10 pretty much what the next book described does for free—but it does include some useful guidelines for short- and long-range financial planning.

College Degrees by Mail: 100 Good Schools that Offer Bachelor's, Master's, Doctorates and Law Degrees by Home Study, John Bear and Mariah Bear. (Berkeley, CA: Ten Speed Press, annual). Our other book on this subject is described on page 132.

College Financial Aid Emergency Kit, Dr. Herm Davis and Joyce Lain Kennedy. (Cardiff, CA: Sun Features, Inc.). A delightful little annual guide that covers much familiar ground, but also deals with renegotiating aid offers, and makes some of the application processes at least appear reasonably simple. Sold by mail for $5.95 from Box 368, Cardiff, CA 92007; (619) 431-1656.

Corporate Foundation Profiles, The Foundation Center. (Irvington, NY: Columbia University Press). This $145 report describes in detail more than 200 of the largest corporate-sponsored foundations in America.

Directory of Athletic Scholarships, Barry and Alan Green. (New York, NY: G. P. Putnam's Sons, 1987). A list of every college and university offering scholarships to men and women in forty different sports, along with valuable advice on how to seek athletic scholarships in both major (football, baseball, basketball, etc.) and minor (lacrosse, field hockey, synchronized swimming, etc.) sports.

Earn College Credit for What You Know, Lois Lamdin. (Chicago, IL: CAEL, 1992). 243 S. Wabash, Suite 800, Chicago, IL 60604; (312) 922-5909. A very useful guide to the preparation of a life experience portfolio.

Financial Aids for Higher Education: A Guide for Undergraduates, Oreon Keesler & Judy K. Santamaria. (Dubuque, IA: Brown & Benchmark, 1994). More than 3,200 programs are listed alphabetically with a good index to help you find things that may be relevant for you. Curious priorities for space, with obscure and tiny grants ($250 from the Jacob's Pillow Dance Festival) getting equal billing with multi-billion-dollar nationwide programs. A new edition emerges every other year, but sadly, with the 11th edition (1984), Dr. Keesler discontinued listings of awards for graduate students. By "sharpening its focus," as he calls it, he has rendered the book much less useful to many. Libraries would be well advised to hang on to their 10th editions, to keep available along with the newer ones.

555 Ways to Earn Extra Money, by Jan Conrad Levinson. (New York, NY: H. Holt & Co., 1992). Described (and endorsed) on page 80 as an inspirational source of ways to earn money to pay for college while in college.

Foundation Directory, edited by Stanley Olsen. (The Foundation Center). New editions every few years. This $195 tome describes more than 3,000 foundations with either assets over $1 million or annual grants over $100,000.

Foundation Grants Index, edited by Ruth Kovacs. (The Foundation Center). An annual cumulation of information appearing in the Center's bimonthly newsletter, plus more than 4,000 additional and new grant descriptions.

Foundation Grants to Individuals, edited by Claude Barilleaux and Alexis Gersunky. (The Foundation Center). Described on page 24 as an excellent source for detailed information on foundations that can award money to individuals for educational and other purposes.

Graduate Scholarship Directory: The Complete Guide to Scholarships, Fellowships, Grants & Loans for Graduate & Professional Study, David J. Cassidy (The Career Press, Inc.). Compiled by the founder of the National Scholarship Research Center, this is a massive 400-page resource.

Independent Study Catalog. (Princeton, NJ: Peterson's Guides, Inc.). In effect a master catalogue, listing all correspondence courses offered by all sixty-nine American universities with correspondence programs.

The Money Book: How to Get a High Quality Education at the Lowest Possible Cost, David M. Brownstone and Gene R. Hawes. (New York, NY: Macmillan). Some good advice on strategies for planning and dealing with colleges and with lenders. Most useful is a "countdown calendar" suggesting the times when it is appropriate to begin saving, planning, applying, etc.

National Guide to Funding in Higher Education. (The Foundation Center). A massive $135 volume set, giving information on each of the more-than-22,000 private foundations in the U.S. that regularly make grants. Foundations are listed by their location and by the amount of their giving, but unfortunately not by the subject areas in which they make grants.

Need a Lift?, edited by K. Michael Ayers. (The American Legion Education Program). This valuable 136-page book appears in a new edition each year, at the amazingly low price of three dollars. About half is devoted to various military and American Legion programs, a quarter to cooperative education programs, and the rest to discussions, charts, and tables covering the more traditional subjects discussed in this book. For $3, how can you go wrong? The book is available at most American Legion posts, and by mail from P.O. Box 1050, Indianapolis, IN 46206-1050, postage included.

Programs in Cooperative Education. (Boston MA: The National Commission for Cooperative Education). A booklet listing all colleges and universities that offer cooperative education programs, in which the student alternates campus time and work for a participating company. Available for $3 from The National Commission for Cooperative Education, 360 Huntington Avenue, Boston, MA 02115-5096; (617) 373-3770.

The Scholarship Book: The Complete Guide to Private-Sector Scholarships, Grants, and Loans for Undergraduates, Michael J. Alves and Daniel J. Cassidy. (New York, NY: Prentice-Hall, 1993). The founder and a former officer of the National Scholarship Research Service, described in Chapter 23, have, in effect, put everything they know about undergraduate scholarships in this book. It consists of a complete reprint of the "databank" of information they use in preparing reports for their clients.

The Student Guide to Federal Financial Aid Programs. A useful free description of GSLs, NDSLs, and other programs described in this book. Available from the Federal Student Aid Information Center, at (800) 433-3243.

An interesting general source of financial aid (and other college-related) information is Octameron Associates. This organization publishes a number of small books and pamphlets with titles like *The A's and B's of Academic Scholarships, The Winning Edge: The Student-Athlete's Guide to College Sports,* and *Campus Daze: Easing the Transition from High School to College,* they have something for just about everyone. The books are somewhat amateurish in writing and design, but the facts are both accurate and useful, and the prices are right (from $4 to $7). They can be reached at P.O. Box 2748, Alexandria, VA 22301; (703) 836-5480.

Chapter
25

Checklists and Maps

Instead of thinking about going to college, let us think, for a moment, about going on vacation. There are interesting parallels which should be apparent in considering the various options:

- You can decide years in advance that someday you want to go to Paris, and start saving up now; or you can impulsively raid the savings account, pawn the jewels, and leave next week.

- You can determine only that you want to go somewhere hot with sandy beaches, but have no idea where. You then study brochures and begin working slowly or rapidly toward a decision.

- You can walk into a travel agent and say, "I've got $2,650 for my vacation; what do you recommend?" or you can say, "I want tour #142-B; here's payment in full."

- You can plan every minute of every day, or you can reach your destination and see what there is to do.

- You may wish to make lists of things you'll need (passport, visas, shots, etc.); what to pack; what to do before leaving home; perhaps where to go, what to bring home, etc.; or you may play it all by ear, and do things as they seem appropriate.

The analogy can be extended indefinitely, including the academic equivalents of sunburn, poison oak, and being fleeced by unscrupulous merchants . . . but you get the point.

Different people will approach the college experience in very different ways, with regard to advance planning, checklists, and roadmaps.

The purpose of this section is to provide a roadmap and a few checklists that may be useful as you plan your quest. They are not essential, but they may help.

The Roadmap

This map is simply a graphic means of looking at the contents of this book. The rectangular boxes are activities you need to do or may wish to do. The ovals are the outcomes of these activities. Following the map will bring you, inevitably and inexorably, to one of the two possible outcomes shown at the bottom.

Checklist for Money

Here are the things you are likely to need or want at some point or points in the process of seeking money for college:

- Your own Personal Financial Statement. There is a standard form for these, and they can be obtained free at most banks, from many accountants and bookkeepers, or bought at stationery stores that deal in prepared forms. The Statement includes detailed listings of all assets, all liabilities, and the current financial picture (income, outgo, insurance, etc.).
- Personal Financial Statements from parents, or anyone else who may be a part of the process, or willing to pay or guarantee payments.
- Last year's federal, state, and local income tax returns. If last year's returns are not yet done, the best advice is to get them done promptly. The second best advice is to accumulate all the significant numbers that will be on the return.
- W-2 forms, and any other evidence of money earned last year.
- Records of nontaxable income, such as welfare, social security, aid to families with dependent children, aid to dependent children, and veterans benefits.
- Current bank statements.
- Records of medical or dental bills paid this year and last year.
- Business and/or farm records. Ledger books, tax returns, profit and loss statements, etc.
- Records of stocks, bonds, and other investments.

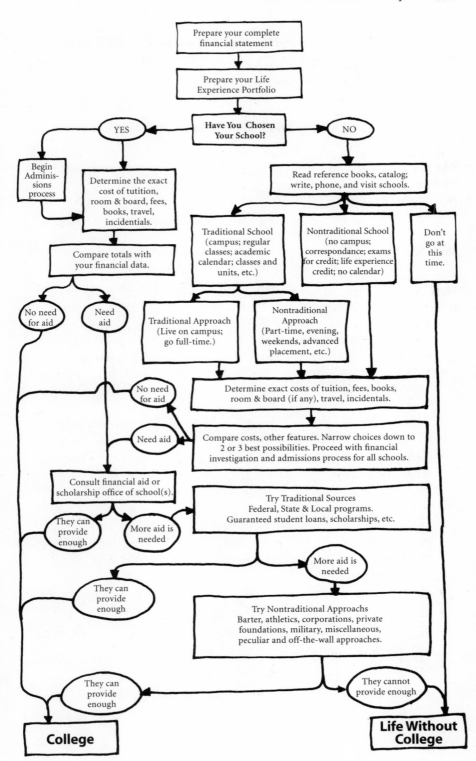

Checklist for Personal Accomplishments

It is desirable to convince both your potential school and potential sources of money that you are indeed a worthy person. The more effectively you present your personal accomplishments, achievements, and skills, the better it will be for you.

Even if you are eighteen years old and have never held a full-time job, there are ways and means of presenting yourself on paper that can help—or hinder—your chances.

And if you are an older person seeking advanced-level entry into a school, or credit for prior learning experiences, the method of presentation can be crucial.

A standard resumé, especially when neatly typed, is a lot better than nothing, but you can almost certainly do better. Better still is a Life Experience Portfolio, which in *addition* to a resumé might include some of the following:

- Letters of reference, especially from people with or for whom you have worked.
- Official or detailed job descriptions.
- Copies of examinations taken.
- Military records.
- Newspaper articles.
- Testimonials and endorsements.
- Slides, tapes, films, videotapes, or photographs.
- Programs of recitals or performances.
- Copies of speeches.
- Licenses (pilot, real estate, etc.).
- Samples of writing, art, or crafts.
- Awards, honors, commendations.

When describing life experience learning, or seeking academic credit for the experience, there are nine categories of experience to consider:

- Academic experience.
- Work. Many job skills also have academic content, and are taught at university level, including typing, shorthand, accounting, map reading, welding, computer programming, editing, real estate appraisal, sales, and many, many others.
- Homemaking. Home maintenance, planning and budgeting, child raising, psychology, education, communication, cooking, etc.
- Volunteer work. Community activities, politics, church work, service groups, hospital work, social service agencies, etc.

- Travel. Study tours, long vacations, study of other cultures, learning languages.
- Recreation and hobbies. Music, aviation, drama, sports, arts, crafts, writing, speaking, gardening, playgoing, concerts, movies, museums, sewing, knitting, and many other leisure-time activities.
- Noncredit formal learning. Company or military classes, in-service teacher training, workshops, clinics, conferences, conventions, lectures, courses on radio or television, etc.
- Private, independent study. Any topic or topics you have read about, or otherwise studied extensively or intensively on your own.
- Talking to experts. Much learning can come from talking to, listening to, and working with experts (credentialled or otherwise), whether in ancient history, carpentry, theology, or Russian folklore.

There is an inexpensive and excellent guide to portfolio preparation: *Earn College Credit for What You Know* (see Bibliography).

Checklist for Time

We have seen books with elaborate and convoluted timelines that start as long as twelve years before you wish to start college, showing what should be done when. In terms of admission, the classic British upper-class tradition of enrolling one's child at the appropriate college of Oxford or Cambridge the instant its sex is known, is hardly relevant for ordinary people. Applying one year in advance is probably the earliest most admissions departments can cope with.

In terms of finances, it's never too early to start setting money aside. Better still, some ancestor started doing so 100 years ago. But aside from increasing your net worth, there is realistically little that can be meaningfully done until about twenty-one months before the day you wish to set foot on campus, and then only if there is discretionary money that can be dealt with so as to have less income and/or *smaller* net worth in the calendar year before applying for aid.

Because both schools and all the many potential sources of money differ so in their policies, procedures, time frames, deadlines, and so forth, the only two items that seem appropriate for a calendar checklist are these:

- Start all financially-related investigations and processes far in advance of any public deadlines, because
- almost everything financial will take longer than you would have believed possible. Estimating the maximum possible time, doubling it, then doubling it again, may be sufficient. Then again, it may not.

Having considered all of the above, we think you're now armed with what you need to go out there and find the money you need for college. We wish you the best in your quest for higher education, and will be interested to hear what you discover along the way, and/or which parts of this book were most helpful. Good luck!

More Innovative Books for Students of All Ages:

College Degrees by Mail
by John Bear, Ph.D. and Mariah Bear, M.A.

It is genuinely possible to earn a legitimate, career-oriented, fully accredited college degree (Bachelor's, Master's, Doctorate, even Law) without spending one semester on campus. This book shows how—by mail, by modem, through exams, and by other methods. Gives full information on the top 100 accredited nonresident schools. Updated annually.

216 pages

Bears' Guide to Earning College Degrees Nontraditionally
by John Bear, Ph.D. and Mariah Bear, M.A.

This directory edition lists over 1,000 schools—the good, the bad, and the unexpected. Programs discussed include wholly nonresidential degrees as well as unconventional residential programs (such as one that allows outdoorsy types to earn a Bachelor's or Master's while bicycling, skiing, and backpacking across America.) Also tells which schools are rip-offs and to be avoided.

336 pages

Major in Success
by Patrick Combs

A hip, fun-to-read guide to making college easier, beating the system while still enrolled, and getting a really cool job when you graduate. Covers how to get into the hot internships, mentorships, and study-abroad programs, lists classes that are worth their weight in gold in the work world, and demystifies the academic world through a series of hot tips.

144 pages

Graduate Admissions Essays—
What Works, What Doesn't, and Why
by Donald Asher

Based on interviews with graduate admissions counselors around the country, this book breaks down how to write an eye-popping essay into a series of simple exercises. Complete with examples of essays that worked in a wide range of fields.

128 pages

For more information, or to order, call the publisher at the number below. We accept VISA, Mastercard, and American Express. You may also wish to write for our free catalog of over 500 books, posters, and audiotapes.

Ten Speed Press
P.O. Box 7123
Berkeley, CA 94707
800-841-BOOK